Tree of
Strangers

Tree of
Strangers

Barbara Sumner

MASSEY UNIVERSITY PRESS

All mothers are daughters.
For Pamela. For Bonnie, Rachel,
Ruth, Amelia and Lilian.

Contents

1

Better call Maysie

R unanga, West Coast, 1983.

I live at the end of a gravel road at the top of a
valley consumed by bush. Beyond our cottage, the
old track has almost disappeared. Gone are the
trucks that once serviced the coalmine. The bush
has closed up behind them like a curtain at the end
of a performance.

I am alone with the wind at night, released by
darkness to rage against itself in our isolation.
Every day the rain engorges the bush with a
lushness that overwhelms our tiny clearing. My
husband is here and my three girls. But the bush
swallows them up like the road, hiding them from
my view beneath a green canopy of enmity.

I wrote those words at the kitchen table in 1983, on a scrap
of paper that survived the many later purges of my life. An
embarrassing early version of an unsent letter to my mother.
The whole world hung on those words. A letter to the mother
I'd never met. The mother I'd dreamed of and longed for. The
mother I had just found. But how do you convey your life in a
few sentences when almost every memory is missing?

It wasn't as if I'd woken from a coma at twenty-three
and found myself stuck in a loveless marriage with three
small daughters. A sleepwalker committing a crime.
I hovered between sleep and waking, unknowing but
somehow not innocent.

Generalised dissociative identity disorder, my
therapist calls it. Generalised because it is not total. I have
fragmented memories: mountain tops poking through
clouds. Dissociative because the physical and emotional
world often feels unreal. Daydreaming on steroids. I forage

for identity or assume new ones, sometimes at the same time. In short, I am an unreliable narrator of my own life.

But diagnosis is good. In adoption circles, we call it 'the fog'.

Mavis and Max, my adopting parents, were instructed to tell me early and to act 'as if' I was born to them. A birth certificate names them as my biological parents. Paper proof of parentage. No one asked what it might mean to adopt a stranger or to be that child. Stripped of meaning or context, 'you're adopted' became a crack in my mind and that's how the fog got in.

Even now I still lose memories as easily as small change. But I remember the night of the phone call.

In Runanga, on the West Coast of the South Island, there was always a storm brewing out to sea. Bruce, my husband, sat in the depths of his chair, his reading lamp held together with tape. We were not television people. Our three girls were asleep in the next room.

The bath was my refuge. I wrapped the plug in a rag and wedged it into the hole. Rusty water struck the pitted cast iron. I sat on the edge of the tub, the chill of the house creeping up, while I waited for the surface to flatten before slipping beneath its perfect skin.

Bruce knocked on the bathroom door. Rain slamming against the window had drowned out the phone. His voice was slow with annoyance. I wrapped a towel around me and went to the kitchen.

'This is Jeannie.' The voice was deep and gravelled.

Almost four years earlier I'd looked into the scrunched face of my first child and seen an inkling of our likeness. It was the first time I'd seen someone I was related to. I wrote to Social Welfare, the first of many letters. A few were recently returned under court order. Held on file through every welfare department incarnation. Sad, pleading messages. Please tell me about my mother. Reading them now, I'm struck by their rawness and intimacy. I imagine the bureaucrats who read them. Their replies were formal. We have no information on your mother. We are unable to help you.

The storm diminished. 'Hi?' I felt like I was shouting down the phone.

'Is that your husband?' Jeannie rushed on. 'Not very friendly, is he?'

'He's reading. He doesn't like the phone much.'

Jeannie's laugh was a short burst of sound, one sharp note on top of the other. I had no idea why I'd told a stranger about my husband.

From the haloed chair Bruce cleared his throat. The moon emerged, casting long shadows across the lawn.

'I'm replying to your letter,' Jeannie said. 'How did you find me?'

Another letter. A random chance that seemed like such a long shot I could hardly believe she was calling.

The library book on finding biological family lost to adoption had advised digging deep to find a dropped clue, a lost memory. Even opening the book had infused me with a sense of disloyalty as indelible as a birthmark. The title is gone. But the stories of lives completed in reunion, the secrets of their stranger adoptions stripped away, brought me to tears. A memory rose up, precise and whole. Mavis's sister had been a nurse for the doctor who delivered me. She was consoling Mavis at the Formica table in our kitchen. I was fourteen and surly.

'What do you expect?' the aunt said, her voice hushed over teacups as I lurked in the hallway. 'Her mother was a model. You've heard the stories . . .' She sucked on her cigarette when she saw me.

It was no more than a crumb.

At the Greymouth library, I took down the Auckland phone book and looked under M for Model. Nothing. But there was a Modelling Society in Wellington.

An extravagant toll call in the calm of early afternoon when the girls were napping and playing.

'Do you know anyone involved in modelling in the late 1950s?' I asked the blithe young woman who answered.

'You better call Maysie,' she said. 'Maysie Bestall-Cohen. You know.'

I didn't know, but Maysie turned out to have been the doyenne of the emerging fashion industry. She sounded kind. The Modelling Society did not get going until the early 1960s, she said. 'Write to Jeannie Gandar, she started everything at the Fashion Fiesta in Upper Hutt in 1961. She knew a lot of girls.'

I wrote to Jeannie at the Wellington Polytechnic, where she taught clothing design. I included a family studio portrait Bruce had won in a raffle. We were standing together in front of a mottled background, new baby Ruth in my arms. Rachel, the middle one, smiling whimsically, while Bonnie gazed down the lens. With nail scissors I trimmed away Bruce and the girls, until I was alone against the painted backdrop. Months passed, and I gave up any hope of a reply. After all it was an impossible task. I possessed just two facts about myself: my date of birth and 'Her mother was a model'.

'I'm replying to your letter,' Jeannie said in her deep voice. 'At first I thought, how ridiculous. It happened to so many girls I knew.' She drew breath and I was sure she was smoking. 'To be honest, I threw your letter away. But something woke me in the night and I thought: That's Pamela's girl. Has to be. The likeness is uncanny.'

My chest tightened. Pamela. Her name is Pamela.

'I got up and drove to my office and saved it from the bin as the cleaners came through.'

I had the impression Jeannie was tall, imposing. The kind of woman everyone noticed. She explained she'd taken months to call because she'd been researching. She'd lost touch with Pamela but found Fred, Pamela's father, living in Waikanae. He remembered the name of the doctor in Napier.

When Jeannie was sure, she'd called Pam in Madrid. Just the word conjured something in me. Madrid. Spain. The opposite of coal-town Runanga with its shuttered mine, roaming dogs and born-again Christians.

'It's remarkable, spooky even,' Jeannie laughed. 'You writing to me, and me knowing your mother.'

'You know my mother.' More wonder than question. My mouth was dry.

'I do. Or at least, I did. You look so like her.'

I'd never felt so tired. 'What should I do now?'

'No need for nerves. Write a letter and send a photo.'

'To Spain?' The idea of mailing a letter from Runanga to Madrid felt impossible. I took down Pamela's address.

'I'll give your letter time to get there, and call Pam back, see if we can arrange a meeting.'

I pressed my forehead to the cold window. Bruce's reading light reflected a bright spot against the native bush that enclosed us. I put down the phone and said nothing.

The bathwater was still hot. I caught my breath as though I was warm and the water cold. My hair floated over the surface and a picture of my mother formed. She would be tall with pale eyes and straight hair that hung thick and glossy, the opposite of my thin plait. I sat up in a rush. I never intended to stay under the water for so long. The stillness induced an amniotic slumber, until a frantic signal from my brain propelled me up, finally desperate for air.

The next morning, with the girls playing, I returned to a

version of the letter that began with the wind and the bush. Outside, in a patch of unexpected sun, I read about our lives. Desperation soaked into every word. I tore the paper into tiny pieces. The chickens consumed the flakes before they realised it was not an early meal.

The next version was more natural.

> *My name is Barbara. I may be your daughter. I have three girls. I married young and had a family to keep from killing myself.*

I started again.

> *We live on the West Coast of New Zealand, in a small cottage. I'm not sure how we ended up here, but it seems to suit us. Bruce, my husband, drives the local bus and makes things from wood, for the tourists who find their way here. He is kind to us.*

Eking out our lives in the middle of nowhere and he is kind to us.

> *We would love to meet you.*

I rewrote the letter in my best handwriting, folded it over another photo and went out to mow the lawn.

What if it was a practical joke? What if Jeannie did not call back? The girls watched from the big window as I forced the push mower through the long wet grass.

Rachel pressed her hand to the glass and it began to drizzle. If only Bruce would take over the mowing. But he was a man of extremes. Bowling greens or wilderness, with nothing in between. So I cut sweeping curves in the overgrown lawn, the blades of the mower clogged with wet grass.

'You're wet,' Bruce said when I came in. The girls were making cushion forts, hungry and niggling each other. Ruth needed breastfeeding. Sharon Crosbie was on the radio, reading a poem cobbled together from weather reports. 'Gusty south-easterlies easing afternoon.' The cadence and beauty struck me. In Runanga, the fine spells were not increasing.

Bruce disappeared to the garage beneath our house to turn wood, the whir of his lathe a distant train coming towards us.

After lunch, I strapped Ruth to my chest and walked the girls to the general store. The postmistress leaned across the counter. Her large breasts flattened on the glass as she held out lollipops.

'Airmail to Madrid. That's in Spain.'

I remember my embarrassment. I wanted to remain separate from these people, and it showed. No matter how I pretended, they considered me a snob. Apart from a slut, it's the worst thing you can be in a small town.

Something outside the valley grabbed my tongue and I could not stop. 'My mother lives in Madrid.' Wind, followed by rain, rattled the front window. 'I'm off to Spain shortly.'

The postmistress glanced from the sleeping baby to the girls holding their lollipops. I'd outgrown the hidden cottage, the tangle of bush and the weather that swept over us like convulsions. Through the fog, I saw a sun-drenched city. There were tree-lined streets and women with pencilled eyebrows in busy cafés. We walked home in the driving rain and I knew it was not my mother I must conjure up. It was me.

2

Cold enough to cut your hair

Was there another phone call? Or did I dream my mother's voice? Did I make it up to soothe the loss? I have lived in two worlds for so long I'm not sure of my own truth.

If you catch me off guard with a question such as: Did you ever speak to your mother? I'll sometimes say . . . Just once. Now, thirty-seven years later, I'm not so sure. Did she call? All the way from Madrid, our lives antipodal, her accent hard to place.

I would have been in the kitchen in our house in Runanga. The scrubbed wooden bench, a coal range and a single gas burner. The peep of sea view sold us on the place. As if that patch of distant blue was enough to banish the isolation. There were chickens, of course, and a goat called Bounce that needed milking at 5 a.m. His idea, my responsibility. Submerged in tiredness. Twenty-three years old and three babies under three.

If she had called, I could have been heating milk to make yoghurt. Or soaking lentils for a nut loaf. Or doing the laundry. The wringer part of the machine had broken. I would twist the nappies around a broom handle and heft the basket outside. On a good drying day the wind would whip the sodden wings into my face while the children watched from the porch. Did I miss her call? My desire was so encompassing I would have believed anything, even my own fantasies.

I'd heard her voice for nine months, her heartbeat, the rush of her blood and the click of her bones. A mother possesses you within herself. And you are secure there. You make a snug cavern of her body, a nest, or a burrow, and it is all yours. She shares everything with you. Her nutrition and discomfort, her anguish and joy, even her temperature. A scientist has described the connection between mother and utero child as like the roots of a tree. Soft villi whiskers sprout from the placenta and delve into the fertile lining of the womb. Branches of the umbilical arteries then carry embryonic blood to the villi. An endless cycle of nourishment.

And we hear voices. In one study pregnant women read a poem out loud. At the sound of the mother's voice, each baby's heart rate quickened. When the recorded voice of a stranger read the poem, their heart rates decelerated. The researcher, Professor Barbara Kisilevsky, said it was not the poem; it was sound. 'They could have read the phone book. We all have our own way of talking,' she said. 'We stop at different times, we take breaths at different times, and that's what the baby recognises.'[1] Would I have recognised my mother on the phone? Voices remain in our sensory memory. After a loved one dies, unless you hear them again through a recording, the memory of their voice will be the first to go.

I have no sensory memory of her. How is it, then, that I am sure of her accent? Her childhood in Manchester and the rush to escape. A handful of years in New Zealand, her life in London and Spain. Her tone and cadence created in those far-flung places.

It does seem plausible that my mother called. Only she didn't.

It was Jeannie who phoned a few weeks after I'd sent the letter. 'She's coming,' Jeannie said, her voice full of cigarettes. 'Your mother is coming. She's leaving soon. I'll call in a few days with the details.'

The next morning I went to the library. I needed to know about the weather in Spain. To picture her there would make it real. In an endless wet summer in Runanga, I wanted to believe in the anointing of sun. The British newspaper made it clear. Unseasonal fog over Madrid. A kata cold front favouring the development of low stratus clouds. Persisting until dawn.

I lingered over those words. Our shared weather. I knew fog. Before Runanga, we lived on a side road beside the Grey River. We'd been there a week when the first fog rolled in. Worst in New Zealand, a neighbour said with pride. The landlord had failed to mention 'the barber'. A katabatic wind, cold enough to 'cut your hair', that invades the Grey Valley most winter mornings.

The night after Jeannie called I went to bed early. For almost a year we had alternated who climbed into the waterbed first. Bruce had insisted on buying it at a garage sale. A singular flourish. In our world such a bed was unknown. Bruce assembled the frame and left me to drag the hose through the window. I'd sat on the floor and watched the water inflate the void with growing dread. The bed was ridiculous, a sign of the desperation that had crept over our lives, specious as neon.

A squall blew in, branches clawing at the side of the house. Jeannie's words played over as the bed settled and the possibility of a real mother filled me.

One of the girls called out, her voice cutting across the ether of longing. Bruce went to her. And I remember thinking I had spent my life hovering between sleep and waking. Fogbound. That perpetual half-life state caused by adoption.

Bruce stood in the doorway, watching me. I should have told him my mother was coming. But the words would not come. He went down to the workshop, a dank space he'd carved for himself, burrowed beneath our lives. The lathe, constant as the sea, drifted up through the floor. He turned wood, piece after piece, shaping chair legs that never matched. Pieces of wood hit the floor with a dull thunk.

I lay in the wash of the bed and thought about the complete unknown of my mother. Not even a photograph.

Closed adoption does this, severing you from yourself. You are a faceless bundle, as devoid of identity as dough. Even with my original name on all the adoption paperwork, my parents denied I'd ever been anyone other than Barbara. The law enabled them. My birth records closed and sealed until after their deaths. Or I turned one hundred and twenty.

It's not only the law that keeps us this way. It's hidden in the words. Adoptee. The '-ee' suffix turns you into an object, someone to whom an action is done. A lifelong sentence. That one word so close to amputee. You are forever an adopted child, infantilised in word and deed, with no rights to your own information. To gain back those early parts of yourself, you must seek a court order. Back when I began to search, they were never approved.

The lathe slowed and Bruce returned, the smell of wood as pungent as aftershave. I felt magnanimous. As though in treading water all my life, my toes had found a little solid ground. But still, I did not tell him.

Jeannie would call again and everything would change. I would take the girls and drive over the Main Divide to Christchurch airport. My mother would walk off the plane and into the terminal and my real life would begin.

Bruce slid into the bed and I touched his shoulder. He curled away, as close to the edge as the waterbed allowed. 'Barbara?'

I hated the way he used my name with polite clarity. The light blond hairs covering the knuckle of his wrist caught the moonlight. The wind died away.

'I saved you.' He said this into the silence, and then he was asleep, just like that.

Years later it occurred to me that this was his talent. His thoughts whittled into one slender, all-encompassing statement. And it was true. Bruce saved Barbara. The defining statement of our marriage. He'd been my way forward, out of the mess of teenage years. Without him, I'd be homeless. Alone in my submerged life, dislocated and abandoned by my parents for the crime of having 'adoption issues'. But his stability was enough for me to begin to shape myself.

How do we remain faithful to the essence of our early relationships and still recalibrate them in a new light? Now I wonder if I was the one who rescued him.

At seventeen I'd crawled through his bedroom window. I fell onto his bed, and into his life, a shipwreck delivered to his harbour. We made our marriage on that rocky shore. I had been his way forward, too, an easy direction. His one grand statement, the perfect comment on his religious upbringing.

I was a bad girl when he had only ever been good. But it had been a seething kind of good. A rankled, angry young man, his virtue worn like a hair shirt that did nothing but plague his skin. I was perfect for him — his salvation, the girl no one would mistake for good. He could relieve his itching without giving up the cause.

The rooster crowed; its call amplified in the pre-dawn dark. I groaned. Every morning the harsh birdcall constricted my chest with exhaustion. I threw the pillow against the wall. As if now, with the imminent arrival of my mother, I could express my dissatisfaction. Some part of me knew this was dangerous. An upset of the unspoken balance between us.

Bruce got up. At the back door, he knocked over the lined-up gumboots. His tread was heavy in the early morning hush. I could hear him stumbling over tree trimmings as he chased the rooster around the bottom of the section. Its crow faded to a frightened squawk, and I wondered what I would wear to meet my mother.

Bruce returned and stood in the doorway, naked apart from his gumboots. The rooster dangled from his hand. Its feet were between his fingers, the head lolling, the bright red comb already dulled. He shook it, and the feathers sighed.

'Happy now?' he asked, and his voice was empty of everything.

3

God fights back

Jeannie rang with flight details while I was making breakfast. My mother would arrive in a week. I told her I'd go to Christchurch to meet her.

Jeannie laughed. 'Good idea. I imagine small-town New Zealand is not her thing.'

I gazed out at the ring of bush and knew it was no longer my thing either.

Bruce was reading in his chair. We'd never discussed my adoption. Devoid of a past, I had always felt insubstantial, a ghost of a person, suspended in a liminal space between identities. It would be years before I understood how humans slide past each other. As if we still bristle with the hair-like villi from the womb, our connections more instinctive than we like to believe. Rabbits sniffing the air to see if it's safe from predators.

But then to some degree we are all predacious. I guess that's why class matters, old school ties, the right neighbourhood, house, clothes, car or accent. We are always assessing each other. Are you one of us?

Adopted people grow up knowing the answer. You come from nowhere. You are strange fruit of obscure origin. The lack of a bloodline marks you. Just ask a mother-in-law. I've had three. For years I wondered why two of them, women from different worlds, treated me with an instinctual distrust. No matter how hard I tried to please them. Now I understand. I was without pedigree, something even a lap dog has. Deep down, they did not want grandchildren without lineage or origin.

Rain-bloated clouds hung over our house. I put down the phone.

'My mother is coming. My real mother.' The words left me breathless.

Bruce looked up. 'I know,' he said. 'I'm not stupid.'

Bounce the goat was tethered outside the living-room

window. She started to wail for her kid. We'd weaned it a few days before and sent it away in the boot of a friend's car.

Bruce gazed out the window. 'The rain's stopped.'

I mixed the batter for muffins. We spent the day in retreat. Perhaps that was the moment the chill overtook us. Later, when the girls were in bed, I ran a bath, locked the door and turned out the lights. The dark was important. Only under its cover could I take off my clothes and uncoil into the hot water.

I undressed in front of the girls. Bruce had observed my body through six years and three children. There had even been a time long ago when we would get naked on the local shingle beach at the height of summer. Or along a tributary to the Māwheranui that once sparkled with gold flakes. It was only alone that I could not endure my body.

Bruce pounded on the door. The sound vibrated through the bath. I guessed he'd been knocking for a while. I let him in and slipped back under the water. He squatted down, curling his fingers over the edge of the enamel.

I could hear the sea in the distance. The first time Bruce found me under the water, he'd grabbed my arm and pulled me out. In fear, I struck him across the face. He'd let go and I hit the side of the bath, blood spouting from my nose.

Now he sat on the floor with his back to the wall. 'It's like you want to drown yourself.'

I tried to explain growing up in a house where they mistrusted privacy. Bedroom doors were always open. Sleeping was in full view with hands above the sheets.

'It's about being whole,' I said. 'For the length of my breath, I'm whole.'

'But you're a mother, doesn't that make you a whole person?' The light from the hallway cast his face in shadow. 'You need help,' he said. 'I've called Jim.'

Jim Doak was the local preacher who believed in the

power of demons. Bruce had begun to attend his meetings.

'Jim will fix you.' His voice was low and soothing, calming a skittish animal.

In the morning, I packed the girls' clothes and placed their bags by the door. I wanted to leave right away, but Bruce shadowed my every move.

Jim arrived after lunch. I'd been expecting a doctor's bag, a box, anything that might contain his magic. But he strode into the living room swinging his well-thumbed Bible. I'd always detested him. The way he parted his hair, slick and precise. And the way he washed dishes after our shared meals, scrubbing at them in a brisk and joyless way as though they were our souls.

Bruce took the girls to their bedroom and set them up with pens and paper. I watched Jim in the reflection from the kitchen window. He nodded toward the couch with the orange-crayoned flower pattern. Bruce returned and we sat together, our knees touching.

Jim positioned himself on the edge of the old armchair. He cleared his throat. 'Thank you, Bruce and Barbara, for taking this step. It can't have been easy.' His smile revealed uneven teeth.

'Barb's a little nervous,' Bruce said.

Jim cleared his throat. 'Could you tell me why you feel the need for spiritual deliverance?'

I remember blushing. 'I don't.' I felt embarrassed and violated at the same time.

'She tries to drown herself.' Bruce grabbed my hand as if it was he who was going under.

Jim leaned forward. 'Drown? How?'

'In the bath. She holds her breath under the water. Like she's unconscious. Like she wants to die.'

'Did you have a bad birth experience?' Jim asked. 'Your own, I mean, not your kids'.'

It was this one question that seared Jim into my memory. It struck me that I had no clue. Growing up, I knew not to mention birth in any way.

My new parents picked me up at ten days old. From where? No one remembers. My legal birth certificate shows my adopters as my birth parents. All other details are blank. My original birth certificate disappeared when I was nine months old and the adoption finalised. I received a copy in 1985 after the Adult Adoption Information Act came into being. But even that supposed original was stamped with the names of my adopting parents. As if I had always belonged to them, even before they trundled my mother into their lawyer's office.

Mavis's memory loss went further. The doctor's name eluded her, even though her sister worked for him for years. She could not remember my mother's name. Years later, when I showed her the papers she'd signed, her signature next to my mother's, she declared them fake.

It was more than memory loss. It was the eradication of my past. As if Mavis and Max alone called me into being at ten days old. There appeared to be no curiosity. No nagging interest about where I came from, who my mother was, my father, my grandparents? I was a warm package delivered by the State, with feeding instructions pinned to a blanket.

Jim turned to Bruce. 'If her birth was traumatic, the water might feel like a safe place.'

I hated that he spoke to Bruce as though I was not there. And that he was right. The bath was my sanctuary, the place of wholeness.

Jim lowered his eyelids. It was a habit that made you think he was deep in thought or prayer. I remember wondering if he was mentally undressing me. Or worse.

'She's never really here,' Bruce said. 'Not when she's caring for the girls.' He paused. 'Or in bed.'

The energy in the room shifted. We were getting down to the main agenda now. Jim explained that Bruce had shared certain things. He inclined his head to signify a touch of embarrassment, and there was a glint in his eye. I stood up, ready to leave, and saw my reflection, devoid of expression, in the mirror above the mantel.

Jim stood in front of me. 'Your past is a little unsavoury.' He seemed pleased with his choice of word.

'Unsavoury how, Jim?' I knew I was not meant to question him. My role was to agree, to be reassuring and give myself up to his wisdom.

'The spirit of harlotry has possessed you, Barbara.' He swallowed as he said it.

I laughed out loud. Jim lowered his voice and told me God had shown him this was the core of my problem.

Bonnie and Rachel stood by the door, holding hands. They had changed themselves into pyjamas, the buttons mismatched. They ran to me and I took them into the kitchen. We would not leave today. I made an early dinner and breastfed Ruth and read them bedtime stories while the men waited in the living room.

'We'd like to pray over you,' Jim said when I returned. 'Our faith in Jesus can deliver you from the demon that is destroying your life.'

When I asked Bruce if he agreed with this diagnosis, he nodded and tried to put his arm around me. Jim flicked through his Bible. I remember saying, Fuck it, deliver me. I wanted it over so I could be on my way.

The men stood each side of me. Jim placed one hand on my forehead, the other in the small of my back. Bruce copied him. I closed my eyes. My head hurt. I wondered for a moment about the feel of thorns. Jim began to pray, imploring God to look favourably upon us.

A laugh rose up from my stomach, like the fits of

giggling that could overtake the girls. The more I laughed, the harder they prayed. Then Jim shoved me, and I fell into his cold-handed embrace. It was like falling under the water. I went with it, sliding into a place where even breathing was unnecessary.

4

The Australia?

Invercargill, 1974.

Sunlight through late summer leaves, a dried-out lawn and a brick fence. We'd moved to Invercargill the year before, and our back yard was bare apart from one tree. Inside the square-fronted stucco house Mavis was ironing. She'd cranked the stereo up to nine as Glen Campbell crooned 'Dreams of the Everyday Housewife'.

I would soon be fourteen. I lay on a blanket and thought: I'm not from this place. Not Invercargill or Whanganui before it. And I wondered if I was even from New Zealand. My life felt as empty as the back yard. I remember all this because I wrote it down in a little notebook I took everywhere. I was beginning to think about adoption, what it might mean and why it made a difference.

I felt it should make me different, like an answer to a question I was yet to verbalise. In the facsimile of a family made by adoption, parents work hard to believe you are *as if* born to them. The law tells you there is no difference. Government-level gaslighting. The Adoption Act 1955 says you are deemed to be the adoptive parents' child as if you had been born to them.

Around that time, Mavis said, 'We love you as if you were ours.' The reply that jumped into my mouth was as dangerous as a bomb: *How would you know?* Years later I understood the cruelty of my response. A clueless child picking at her scab of infertility. It caused a week of glacial silence, presaging the silences to come whenever I questioned adoption.

When we are young, most of us think our childhoods are normal. Adopting families are as diverse as any other. Conditional and unconditional. How was I to know that in this one my behaviour was the arbiter of love? When I was good, it was down to their parenting, and the warmth flowed. When I misbehaved, it was all in my genes, as if I'd inherited nothing from my mother except her immorality.

To paraphrase Tolstoy, every family is miserable in its own way. But with many adoptions, conditional love plays into an understory of abandonment and rejection. Today they would say I had Adopted Child Syndrome. A kind of psychopathology leading to all manner of negative social behaviour. Back then all I wanted was to escape.

The longing under that tree in the back yard was so intense I thought I had called him to me. Leon. The love god of James Hargest High School. I opened my eyes and he was there, blocking the sun, the boy every girl at school wanted. He knelt down. So far, our courtship consisted of him once taking my hand at the bus stop and walking to band practice. I'd sat on an upturned beer crate in a filthy garage while the boys tried to play in time.

'Nice music,' Leon said as Glen Campbell moved on to 'If You Go Away'. 'Do you want to go away?' he asked.

I'm sure I nodded and he suggested Australia. He said it fast, as if that would reduce the immensity of the idea.

'*The* Australia?' My cousin had run away there the year before. It became the latest family secret, spoken in hushed tones.

Leon said he had tickets for the next day. His bandmates were sure I'd refuse. I tried to stand up but my back hurt and he held out his hand. I told him I had $20 from babysitting, and he asked what I was saving it for. 'This trip,' I said. 'When do we leave?'

He smiled with the sun behind him and told me he knew I was different. The plan was to meet at the school gates, walk to the depot and catch a bus to the airport. Back then Kiwis could go to Australia without a passport. But we needed more money.

That night I dreamed I was wearing every piece of clothing I owned, limbs stiff as scarecrows'. In the morning

Mavis's handbag was on the kitchen bench. Her purse bulged with the weekly housekeeping, enough to feed a family of four. We were going shopping after school to buy the shoes I'd been saving for. The fold of notes seemed to jump into my pocket.

Leon was waiting at the school gate. A friend punched him on the arm. I had pins and needles down my leg, and the fingers that stole the money were numb. Leon's hair needed washing. I thought about going home. I could pretend to be sick, then slip the money back in her purse and lie down on the floor to relieve my sore back.

But Leon held my hand. It felt as if the whole school watched us leave.

My family had moved every two or three years. From Napier to Invercargill to Upper Hutt to Westport, back to Upper Hutt and to Whanganui. I was always the new girl, always the outsider, always moving on. We'd been back in Invercargill a few months and I had no friends. I knew going with Leon would mark me and not in a good way. We walked to the bus depot and changed out of our uniforms. I looked in the toilet mirror and mouthed hello as if I was someone I'd just met.

Outside I took his hand, wet from slicking back his hair. 'I'm adopted, you know,' I said as the bus arrived. We slung our school bags over our shoulders and stood at the end of the line.

'What does that mean?' Leon asked.

'They chose me.' I saw babies lined up like fruit and Mavis squeezing their chubby thighs. Our turn came to board and Leon let go of my hand.

'Let's get a milkshake,' he said. 'My favourite is strawberry.'

We walked to the dairy as though we were foreigners, tourists from afar. Leon told me things. About being in the band and how inside himself he could play anything. But in the garage it came out wrong. About his parents and his younger sister who got all the attention. And the operation that meant he could not play cricket.

We walked around a park near the school. When I went to drink from a tap, he cupped his hands and I sucked the water from his palm. We found a hidden recess of branches behind a gardener's shed. I remember the lacey foliage and how weightless I felt, the grass beneath like a Lilo floating over a pool.

He kissed me, his lips dry, the moisture sucked away. I gave myself up to it, the Lilo floating out to sea, the water warm and gentle around us.

Leon rolled off before I knew what his weight on me had meant. He placed his hand on my belly where he had pushed up my top. Later in my notebook I wrote that if you added up the hours, we'd known each other for less than a day. I wondered out loud if we could only tell our secrets to strangers.

'So the more you know someone, the less you tell them,' Leon said.

I thought about how my parents communicated by looks over our silent dinner table.

'What should we tell people?' he asked, all his bravado gone.

The floating feeling turned to heaviness. 'Nothing. That way it will always be a mystery.'

The school bell rang in the distance and we changed back into our school uniforms. Needles of pain shot down my leg. The discomfort had begun the year before. Growing pains, Mavis said every time I complained.

I walked home along the wide and treeless street, trying not to limp. I planned to put the money back in her purse when she was in the toilet before we went shopping. As I neared the house, I could see the windows shut tight, despite the warmth of the day. Inside the light seemed dusty, diffused through the net curtains. I walked down the hall, arms extended, fingers tingling as I traced the wallpaper pattern. For the first time, I thought the place lovely.

She was at the kitchen table, the ashtray full. The teacup in front of her was stained with lipstick, half-empty, filmed over and cold.

They say losing your mother at birth encodes trauma in your pituitary sensory system. You become hypervigilant. To stay safe, you observe and copy your new parents' behaviour. I was adept at following the mood of any room, the slightest whisker shift enough to put me on high alert.

But that day there was no need for hypervigilance. Mavis stared at me without a trace of warmth. I was too afraid to speak. 'The school called. You were absent all day. The principal said you were planning to go to Australia. With a boy.'

I remember crying and how warm and pleasant the tears felt. I denied it all, gulping, caught up in my own wounded tone. I spread my fingers over the Formica and wondered about the money.

The slap came as I glanced toward her purse. My face stung. 'You're a liar.' She grabbed my fingers and squeezed them till I thought they'd break.

'You're hurting me.'

'No. It is you who are hurting me.' She dug her nails into my wrist till I yelled. When she let go, she opened her handbag and held it open in front of my face.

'What am I supposed to be looking at?' I must have smiled then as she slapped me again.

'Your father will have something to say about this.'

'You wouldn't blame me if I weren't adopted!' I kicked a chair and sent it spinning across the polished lino. The words that had piled up inside me came spilling out. 'I'm not like you. You tried to force me, but I'm someone else.'

She turned as Max stood in the doorway. He walked past me and took his wife's hand as if I was not there, and led her from the room.

In my bedroom, I closed the door and adjusted the venetians. Late afternoon sunlight hit the blinds, brightening the edges of each slat. I imagined myself a swimmer. I would live under the sea, in the cavern of a crusted ship, while above the storm subsided, the surface turning glassy and tranquil.

The light faded and hunger overtook me. When I stood, pain shot down my leg and along my arms and I fell and could not get up. I called for help but no one came and I lay on the floor unable to move as the night came on.

5

Another kind of memory

Runanga, 1983.

When I came to, I was on the floor. Jim and Bruce were kneeling over me, imploring their God to free me from the spirit of harlotry. My teenage self disappeared. It was dark and all I could see were our reflections in the big window. Three hopeless people surrounded by the blackness of the night. I felt a pain deep in my chest, a sense of time running backwards. Past the birth of my three girls. Beyond my unmoored life before Bruce. Back further than the flattened plain of childhood. To memories that were not memories.

With closed stranger adoption you have no birth story, as if you exist by magic alone. But that day, on the worn carpet in my lounge, the story of my birth rushed at me. As if I'd actually been there. As if my mother and I were one. I have never experienced that exact feeling again, but the story stayed with me.

It began with drizzle, a dark corridor and an image of curtains, luminous as mist. A woman I knew was my mother stretched her hands towards a baby in a stranger's arms. The curtains were like wedding veils between them. I was then in an old graveyard. She was sitting in a white-painted portico surrounded by mossy gravestones. She wore a coat that did not cover her belly; her eyes were closed against the slant of the early winter sun.

Beside the graveyard, the city fathers (never the mothers) had planted a park on the sides of a gully. Low walls of volcanic stone led down to a grassy meadow. I found myself walking along those paths as if I was my mother, the baby that would be me heavy within her. The moo of cows drew her on. She dozed against a tree, watched by the cows, curious and indifferent. When she woke, it was dark. The baby curled tight inside, calm for once. She held the weight of her belly and trudged back up the steep path. The restless cows ran to the edge of their meadow, their breathing heavy behind her.

Her name was Pamela. She was tall and auburn-haired. In the photo above my desk she is modelling swimwear. She looks right down the lens, all eyeliner and the puffy hair of the early sixties. She was nineteen when I was born, a vulnerable new immigrant from London. Her parents were here too. On the evidence of her belly, her father, Fred, had thrown her out of their new home in Tawa. Her mother, my grandmother Jessie, was dying from breast cancer.

On the day she went into labour an anticyclone covered the country. A slow-moving depression deepening in the east, bringing fog and low cloud.

Mesmerised on the lounge floor in Runanga I saw a doctor take her arm. He led her past a nursery of swaddled babies. When one began to wail, the child inside her shifted. In a windowless room at the end of the corridor, she removed her faded dress. She slid her arms into a gown washed almost transparent, climbed onto a narrow bed and pulled up the sheet.

In the late stage of pregnancy you are lethargic and drenched in dreams. I imagine her facing the wall, whispered incantations rising from heart to mouth. She tells her baby everything as the contractions merge, propelling me from her.

And there my dream state ends.

I've had four children, so what comes next is easy to imagine. The way a contraction rises up, feathery as a shadow, stealthy as a rogue wave. Each surge breaks through the silent conversation you've been having with your baby. It is only as your body splits itself in two to expel the child that you understand what it means to be pregnant. To hold life within and feel it grow till it might break through your blue-veined skin.

I want to think we had some time together. On the outside, as it were. That I lay in the curve of her naked body, my mouth inching instinctively toward her breast.

But I think she woke in an empty room bright with light, groggy from the drugs they would have given her. She was alone on a distant beach far above the high-tide line with the sure knowledge her baby was gone. Removed from her bruised body as if it never belonged there. As if *I* had had no right to be there.

Was it Dr Gerald Gleeson who took me from her? By the time he retired, he'd delivered ten thousand babies. He was the doctor of the day for the good married ladies of Napier. In his general practice, he discussed their infertility. In his obstetric practice, he canvassed for the cure. Young, single, pregnant women were the answer.

Women like my mother. With three months to go, her parents sent her to stay with Dr Gleeson and his wife. A woman who knew the doctor described him to me as a friendly man who let women birth without their legs in stirrups. She'd been to dinner at his house but seen no sign of pregnant girls scrubbing and cleaning.

But the files don't lie. It's clear they put my mother to work cooking and cleaning the three floors of the Gleesons' large house on Hospital Hill. He'd trained as a priest and I'm told he was surprisingly light on his feet for a man of his size. Not tall, but heavyset, his white coat only ever partially buttoned. Reading the doctor's obituary, you get the impression he was a man in his element among grateful women.

Or perhaps it was the matron, Brigadier Gladys Goffin, who took me away. She ran the Salvation Army Bethany home in Napier for twenty years. An article in the local paper described her as preaching hellfire and damnation that left you shaking in your shoes. 'She could prompt soul-searching in even the most self-righteous', and believed unmarried girls 'drifted' into pregnancy because of aimless lifestyles.[2]

It hurts me to imagine my mother condemned and shamed for getting herself pregnant, my father as blameless and distant as a deity. It's easy to see how the pious doctor and the self-righteous Brigadier could destroy my mother's hopes and dreams.

Twenty-five years later, in a heartbreaking letter, my mother's husband described my adoption as forced. New Zealand was unforgiving and unrelenting, he said. Pamela was so confused by what had been done to her that she had a nervous breakdown following her loss. 'The scars never left her,' he said.

Under the Adoption Act 1955 a mother cannot consent to the adoption of her child until it is ten days old. Ten short days to decide to give away or keep your baby. For those days every mother in New Zealand, married or single, has sole legal custody of her child.

Every unmarried mother I've spoken to says her baby disappeared. Straight from her womb or shortly after delivery. From across the country, the mothers' stories echo each other. Their babies taken and concealed in other parts of the hospital as they were readied for adoption. On day ten, the matron escorted the mother to an office where a lawyer read a general waiver out loud. With matron standing behind, they signed away their babies. Not one had legal representation.

I now think of the ten-day provision as the basis of the idea that mothers willingly gave away their babies. It was a whitewash. A way to hide the mechanics of the adoption industry in New Zealand.

Back in my living room in 1983 with Jim and Bruce, I scrambled up from the floor. My breathing was shallow with my mother's pain. I am sure I saw the pallid curtains part. I am convinced she reached for me as a woman with black hair turned in alarm, the baby she held tight already hers.

Bruce put a blanket around my shoulders. Jim took up his guitar and began to sing.

> *Something beautiful, something good,*
> *All my confusion He understood*
> *All I had to offer Him was brokenness and strife.*
> *But He made something beautiful of my life.*

The music woke Bonnie and Rachel, and they came and sat with me and we sang together. Ruth would be awake soon for her first feed of the night.

I thought about each of their births. I could pick their cries in a crowded room. I could sense every shift in mood, even a change in their body temperatures. Scientists say oxytocin, the motherhood hormone, causes this heightened awareness. Researcher Robert Froemke says oxytocin enables a mother to understand her baby's needs '[b]ecause your baby depends on you absolutely to take care of it'.[3]

I know I am biologically wired to my children and that the wiring persists long past childhood. Now my daughters are adults with lives and families of their own. But I am still wired to them in ways that defy logic. Did my mother hear my cries from the distant nursery? I can hardly bear to imagine the pain she must have felt.

But then, so early in my journey, I remember how Bruce hugged Jim and thanked him. Jim smiled at me distantly and raised his hand. 'I hope that helps,' he said. I gathered myself and put the girls back to bed and washed the dishes.

Bruce returned to his chair. His face was already going soft. His halo of hair needed cutting. I was no longer mad at him. This was as far as we could go. We had found the outer rim of our emotional compatibility. I thought about the way time had rushed backwards beneath the men's prayers. In some unspoken way I'd always felt that without a past I could have no future. 'It's like I've been paralysed my whole life,' I said to Bruce.

He'd already opened his book. He looked up and nodded. 'Do you feel better?' he asked.

Strangely, I did. I felt lighter, with my mind resolved. Perhaps the spirit of harlotry had forsaken me after all. Without a past I only had now. I would leave in the morning. My mother was coming.

6

The changeling

Before the curtains bloomed with morning light, I had milked the goat and made sandwiches. While the girls ate their porridge, I filled the car with clothes, toys and food. Bruce watched in silence from the safety of his chair. Beneath the girls' chatter, stillness settled over us. While the words remained unsaid, he was innocent. He'd done his best, even called in the preacher. He could live in the comfort of his wife's betrayal. The act of leaving would be all mine.

I strapped the girls into their car seats. Bruce leaned in to kiss them. He cried and I touched his face. 'Wait,' he said, and went into the house.

He came out and held up my favourite, almost-antique platter. I had served countless meals on it, gravy consuming the faded blue patterns. It had been missing from its usual place. Now I understood. He had hidden it so he could present it now, a peace offering, a show of support, to win me back.

He opened his hands and the platter slipped from his fingers and shattered on the concrete. He looked right through me. I was beyond his redemption but not his retribution.

'You can't have them, or any of this.' He swept his hand over the car, kissed my cheek and told me to drive with care.

'Wave to Daddy,' I said. But Bruce had already gone inside and the girls turned in their seats and waved to the blank eyes of the house.

We drove away and Bonnie asked why I'd upset Daddy. 'You shouldn't say bad things to him,' she said.

The question stunned me. How did she know that deep down I believed this was my fault, my character flaw, my genetic defect?

Adoption can do this to you. From the beginning you are 'a' child. But you are not 'the' child, the one they longed for and could not have. And despite everyone's best efforts, you are never quite right, because in all kinds of love we look for a mirror, a reflection, a version of ourselves. The parent–child relationship is no different.

You start out as a warm weight to fill the empty arms. But as you grow with no resemblance to your new parents you become the *other*.

Of course, all children transform into other as they become themselves. As parents, we shepherd that transformation. But the mythology around adoption says that there is little difference between a natural child and an adopted one because you raise them up the same. So natural differentiation is hampered, even squashed, to keep the myth of sameness alive. As you slip between being the desired baby and being the stranger in their midst, your identity becomes a constant and often unconscious internal negotiation. Until you have children or meet family in reunion. It is often at this point that you realise you've been looking for someone you resemble your whole life and that you begin to understand genetic mirroring.

Biological families never get to question mirroring. It's as natural as air. Parts of you are reflected in the people you see every day. It goes beyond physical resemblance.

In reunion with biological families, adopted people speak of the shock of the mirror. How strange it is to recognise an inflexion or the rise and fall of a laugh. A matching earlobe or a subtlety of language. In these moments we begin to comprehend what the adoption myth denies.

I've heard reunion described as shedding a skin. But what if I sloughed off my salamander skin, translucent as milk, to find there is nothing beneath? This fear of being without substance in form or function haunts me still.

But consider the newly minted adoptive mother. What does she see when she gazes into the eyes of the child most longed for? She will not find her reflection there, not even a scrap of similarity. The new baby is as much the other to her as she is to it. A part of her knows this is not her baby.

Historically, women who gain motherhood with someone else's baby occupy an uncomfortable place in society. In folklore, elves or fair folk took the rightful child and replaced her with one of their own. The changeling child. In Rumpelstiltskin, a woman in fear of her life must promise away her firstborn to survive. An ugly troll takes her baby. In Rapunzel, a husband offers up their future child to save his wife. The one who returns to claim the eventual child is of course an evil witch. Even the Bible gets in on the act. Moses' mother must choose between her son being killed or letting an Egyptian princess raise him. When two women claim a newborn as their own, King Solomon threatens to divide the baby in two. It is the real mother who is willing to give up her child to save it.

The message has always been that only dire circumstances will part a mother and her child. And those who take advantage of that situation are never real mothers.

But even now, all these decades later, I know Mavis's heart's desire was to be *the* mother and not just a mother. Despite her discomfort, she wanted to love the baby she ended up with. But she had to bond without the help of hormones. Without the oxytocin released in breastfeeding. Without nine months of the shared journey, or the element of the mystical that lingers over birth. An adopting mother must nurture without the welcome home from the travails of childbirth, without celebration or the sense of ancestors hovering nearby.

In the absence of those ancestors she must pour herself into that void. She must grow her love based on need alone — hers to be a mother and the child's need for care. And she must believe, above all else, in the power of nurture over nature.

In a moment of weakness, Mavis once confessed that

she felt everyone knew she was not a real mother. She feared the opinion of other women and the censure of her fecund sisters. She had to be above reproach in all the ways we judge mothers. She over-compensated, orchestrating every detail of our lives. From perfect homemade clothes to perfect hair and the expectation of exemplary behaviour. I was always under scrutiny. Any hint that nature might claim me back was crushed.

But then I became a teenager, a true changeling. There were cultural and emotional differences that nothing in my upbringing could explain. It was in that failure of nurture to create a likeness that our adoption myth began to unravel.

My wrongness was like a mine shaft that swallowed up all my self-esteem. And then there was my other wrong. The one that set me apart.

My spine first gave out at thirteen. For almost two years no one believed I was in pain. I finally collapsed that night in the bedroom, unable to move even a finger without unbearable spasms. A genetic defect, they said over and again until those words came to define me. The damage was such that surgery was urgent and expensive. There was a chance of permanent disability. I was in bed for months as Mavis cared for me as a good mother does.

But such was the power of those two words 'genetic defect' that no one thought to enquire further. Spondylolisthesis was, after all, an inherited lumbar weakness. The perfect explanation for all that was wrong with me. I was forty-nine when a doctor administered a shockingly painful inter-muscular injection and the memory returned.

A warm summer afternoon in Whanganui the year I turned twelve. I climbed out of my bedroom window and walked around the new subdivision that had sprung up nearby. The pine forest they'd toppled in a week had been my solace. Now I scrambled through half-built houses. I climbed on the wheel of a resting bulldozer to look at the picture of a naked woman taped to the ceiling. I returned home an hour later, walking through the back door as if I belonged there. Mavis did not look up. The set of her shoulder was enough to tell me a cold front was passing through our kitchen. I had to wait in my bedroom with the lemon striped wallpaper. Max arrived already angry, the leather strap in his hand. But I was thirteen and beginning to feel my boundaries. I must have argued with him, and he picked me up and shoved me against the wall. The exact moment my back gave out, the genetic weakness activated by blunt-force trauma.

F or all those years I'd hidden that memory. My defect the perfect example of essential wrongness. Years later, even my four-year-old knew it. I had angered Daddy. It was all my fault.

We drove past the general shop and the petrol station. 'When will Daddy fix your plate?' Bonnie asked.

I kept my voice soft as I explained that some things were unfixable.

I'd taken to using a placating singsong voice with them when they asked the difficult questions. I caught myself doing it again. From then on I determined always to speak clearly. To be a different kind of parent. The kind who did not paper over everything uncomfortable.

'My mother is coming,' I said in my new serious tone. 'We're going to meet your grandmother. We are on our way.' And I knew then I was going home. A metaphorical home. And I imagined us leaving with my mother, flying to Spain to start again. The idea felt as unreal as footprints after the tide.

We drove over Arthur's Pass. Bonnie and Rachel argued

over the colour of a horse. Or whether it had been a cat or a dog sitting in front of a house. We stopped for lunch at a roadside table. I unpacked the sandwiches while the girls explored the edges of the clearing. Ruth staggered after them on her baby legs. They looked under bushes and chased each other. I watched them from the picnic table as they huddled over a dead bird. Bonnie pushed it with her toe. Rachel jumped and squealed while Ruth sat down to touch it. Bonnie waved, pointing to the dead bird. Would she remember this moment? Or would it become part of the blur of childhood? As normalised as the everyday violence of the leather strap and the cold shoulder.

The girls fell asleep as soon as we left, their heads lolling over the sides of their seats. I rolled the car wide around the corners so as not to disturb them. Anything to prolong the quiet. We drove through a tunnel and I thought about ghosts. The spectral image of my mother leaning over her lost baby. And the ghost I had become. I'd been living between two worlds. In a couple of days, I would take my mother's hand and we would step out of the fog and into the sunlight.

7

And the dolphins walked on water

The sun came out as the countryside gave up its green. When the girls woke I put in a tape and we sang along to Joni Mitchell's song about paving paradise. Christchurch still made me nervous. Another life before marriage and children and rural bliss. A world of damp squats and the Jesus movement.

We stopped at the lights near the motel, and I realised this was the very corner they caught me, a few weeks before I turned seventeen. A group of people had gathered around a short man who, dressed in homespun clothes and with shaggy hair, looked as though he'd escaped a hippy commune. An older woman smiled, and that was enough to pull me in. His name was Marcus Arden. He waved his arms as he told a story about driving across the Desert Road on his way to an important meeting. A snowstorm came out of nowhere and the road became impassable. Marcus prayed, and God parted the snow as easily as water and he drove on.

Now I understand it as an acid trip, repackaged for a new audience of broken people. But then it sounded like a miracle. He was part of a group of men, including Jim, who proclaimed themselves saviours of the true faith. And especially the saviours of women like me. Except I was a child pretending to be an adult. Living on the streets some of the time, or staying with a cousin. Those were dangerous days. Filled with street drugs and the kind of iniquity the Jesus movement flourished on.

Marcus led us through the Square in the middle of old Christchurch. The beautiful city before the earthquakes swallowed it all. He stopped in front of the Cathedral and preached about the evils of organised religion. Nearby his friend Ray Comfort perched on a small ladder and yelled at the pigeons and the passersby. Ray was natty and sharp-edged, convinced of his rightness. He was the opposite of Marcus, who tended to bumble and mix his words. Except when preaching. The men acknowledged each other, and Ray winked. We followed Marcus along the street and down the stairs to the Love Shop.

I'd heard about the drop-in centre on the streets. Free tea and a change of clothes. There were piles of tracts written by Ray, with stick figures illustrating the effects of sin. Marcus took me aside. He'd seen the same evil spirits that would so excite Jim a few years later. The month before, three men I didn't know had hustled me into a car. They drove around with the doors locked and took me to a house near New Brighton beach. The details of the weekend they held me are fuzzy and razor sharp at the same time.

Marcus and then Ray were keen for all the details. They rebuked me for allowing such sin into my life. They believed that we must each take responsibility for the hell that happens to us. I'd strayed from God's path and into the clutches of evil. I was a rich seam of transgression that only prayer could fix. Even as I confessed my sins, it seemed strange that it was up to God to bring the perpetrators to justice. But then, it was 1976 and the end times were upon us.

'Are you ready to die for Jesus?' Ray Comfort asked. I said I was, but not in a sacrificial way. No one thought to ask what I meant. To them, I was a new convert and that was enough.

But at that very point I *was* ready to die. It never once occurred to me that wanting this might be related to adoption. An article published by the American Adoption Congress says it best: 'Adoption is created through loss; without loss, there would be no adoption.'[4] The authors describe how young people struggle to grieve for their losses. And how adults can block or divert expressions of pain. Delayed grief, they say, may lead to depression, substance abuse or aggressive behaviours. If you strung adoption loss on a washing line it would cover the hills and valleys of your life. It is no wonder adopted people are four times more likely to attempt suicide.[5]

Now I know. Now it makes sense. I was an adolescent, too young and too old for my age. Those teen years are the time when you test the beliefs and goals acquired from your parents. An organic process. A natural progression. But somehow I'd missed each step. I had no idea what my adopting parents believed. They'd shared so little of themselves. The few stories that escaped the silence felt unreal. Someone else's stories. And you did not ask questions. Most of all you did not talk about adoption. The few times I tried, the answer was always the same. We know nothing. They did not tell us your name or her name. They struggled to articulate the idea that I had come from another woman's body. A phantom child from a phantom mother. Your mother's name. The void created by their secrecy was big enough to hide a body.

Six months after the spinal surgery I left home. They let me go without fuss or question. A small boat untethered on a high tide. No wonder I followed those arrogant men with their vocal passions and beliefs. Later I understood their preaching was more dangerous than the streets.

And then Bruce came along. He was on the run from his Baptist parents. From a father who berated tardy parishioners in the street and a mother who gave up dancing to meet her husband's needs.

Bruce bought an old bus and we drove away from Christchurch. The red scar that ran fresh down my spine and across my hip fascinated him. He did not care that my identity was so fragmented or that I had no history beyond the last few months. Neither of us had a coherent sense of self or any idea of a future.

We decided to drive to Kaitāia in the far north, using only the back roads. We were quiet with each other. Incurious and unquestioning. Safe. On the way we stopped in Napier. We parked on Marine Parade and I could hear the dolphins calling.

When I was a child, Mavis and Max took me to Marineland. I wore a yellow sunhat and watched the dolphins swim in circles. They jumped through flaming hoops and sang on command. They flapped their tails and 'walked' on water. When the show was over, they sank beneath the surface and returned to swimming in circles. Their trainers laughed and bowed. We clapped and cheered their ability to make the animals perform. The more unnatural the better.

I would lie awake at night and think of ways to rescue the dolphins. A helicopter with a net, a truck with a tank. The helplessness of their situation flooded into my dreams. Did I make the connection between their truncated lives and my own? The loss of their natural habitat, behaviours, families and culture? Not in any conscious way. And yet every night I swam in those same circles, the cement walls closing in.

The girls were impatient. We were lost and I had to drive around looking for our motel.

'Are we going to see our new grandmother today?' Bonnie asked.

I checked the time. My mother would be on her way. Every part of me longed to call her Mummy. I had never called Mavis that. A therapist would call it a trigger word.

'Not today, my love. Two more sleeps.' I tried not to cry. 'Two more sleeps and my mummy will be here.'

'My mummy,' Bonnie and Rachel chimed together. Ruth started to whine. 'Her nappy is wet,' Rachel said.

We parked outside the motel. I carried Ruth on my hip and the older girls acted as if they travelled and stayed in motels all the time. The place looked nothing like the brochure I'd picked up at the library. Instead of tall pines, over-pruned shrubs surrounded the dried-out lawn. The pool was a misshapen dent. I had built up an image of staying somewhere flash. A movie motel with palm trees and cocktails around the pool. I had enough money from our savings for three nights in a dump.

A thin woman with a shaved head answered the buzzer. I wondered if she was the shrub pruner. She glanced at the girls with distaste.

'It'll be extra for the children,' she said. I was about to argue, but the plastic plant and faded posters of the Riviera stopped me. I imagined the woman in plumper days. Flushed with enthusiasm for her little business as she balanced on a stool to hang the posters.

I smiled at her and thought how proud my mother would be of a daughter who was kind to people in distress. I counted out the money. 'It's a nice pool, isn't it girls,' I said to seal the deal.

'Can we swim right now?' Bonnie asked in her most grown-up voice, and her sister echoed her.

'Room's other side of the pool,' the woman said, and handed over the key.

Standing in front of the motel door, assailed by the smell of chlorine, I looked around. It was a beginning.

The woman called out across the courtyard. 'Mrs.' She flapped a scrap of paper. I winced. I was too young to be a Mrs. I let the girls into the room and dashed around the pool.

'He said it was important.' She handed over the note. 'I didn't catch what he was saying.'

She'd written Bruce's name in lower case as if a capital letter was more than a man deserved.

I had no intention of calling him. 'Too little too late,' I said and smiled and the woman's face softened in our complicity.

In the room, the girls were fighting over the beds. I thought about calling home, to let him know we were safe. But I didn't want to hear the accusation in his voice, the blame in the gaps between his words. I would call him later. After a swim, after I'd unpacked the car and made dinner with the food from home. He could wait.

The promise of a swim sent Bonnie and Rachel careening around the room. But Ruth pulled her legs to her chest, refusing to let me change her. I loved how determined she was, so resolute, even at fourteen months old.

The phone rang as we went out the door. The girls were already near the gate, dragging their towels over the hot concrete. It will just be him, I thought, and remembered how he'd saved my life. He'd given me children who kept me afloat. He had given me reason and purpose. And now I was leaving him. I picked up Ruth and let the phone ring on in the empty room.

8

The opposite of Easter

The girls finished their swim and we went to Piko Wholefoods for fresh fruit. The weather report played on the radio behind the counter. 'A foehn wind, warm and dry, has formed to the west in the Zone of Calms.' I smiled. The Zone of Calms was perfect for this day. It felt like the weather reporter was speaking only to me. 'But don't forget,' he added, 'all winds are liars: they never blow from the exact quarter whence they come.'[6]

'Did you hear that?' I asked the man waiting behind me. He was large and round with sparse hair. 'I did.' He had the kindest smile. 'Typical National Radio. Even the announcers think they're actors. That part about the wind is Greek philosophy, I think.'

He had a lovely voice. 'You sound like an actor. Or you could be on the radio,' I said.

He inclined his head, and his eyes crinkled with warmth as he helped put the fruit on the counter. 'Nice girls,' he said and patted their heads.

They clamoured for lollipops. I planned to break that habit now we were away from the postmistress. But I gave in and we drove back to the motel in peace.

I could hear the phone as we walked past the pool. The girls wanted to swim again. Anger at Bruce's persistence welled up.

But it was Jeannie. 'I found you. Bruce gave me the name of the motel.' She sounded as though she had been running.

I laughed. 'We decided to come a couple of days early, to be on the safe side, in case the car broke down.' I could hear an echo in my voice. Something was wrong. I wanted to keep talking, to fill up all the gaps so she could not speak. The girls were in the next room, fighting over the towels, and I could hardly hear over their screams.

'Hold on.' I closed the door to the bedroom and lay down on the couch and cradled the phone against my ear.

'Let's start again. Hi, Jeannie.'

'Bad news.'

I remember my fingers spread over my chest. The yelling from the bedroom intensified and then fell silent. My mother had changed her mind. She did not want me after all. I had no right to expect anything else.

Jeannie began to cry. Breathless sobs that drenched the gravel in her voice. I could not understand why she was crying. This was my loss, not hers. My brain switched to organisation mode. The curse of resilience, of glossing over emotion to ensure survival. I was never sure if it was flight or fight. Or perhaps it was freeze mode. The stagnation of all emotion.

'Okay,' I said. 'Maybe next year. Or the year after. It was probably too quick for her.'

'No,' Jeannie whispered. 'That's not it. Her plane. It was on the news. On the radio. There was fog. On the runway. Her plane was taking off.'

All winds are liars. 'There's been a mistake. It must be a mistake,' I said. But the weather report I'd read at the Greymouth Library had mentioned unseasonal fog over Madrid. A kata cold front favouring the development of low stratus clouds. Persisting until dawn.

'Her poor girls,' Jeannie said.

'What girls?'

I could hear Jeannie's footsteps as she walked away. She blew her nose and came back.

'I'm here,' she gulped. 'Her daughters. I was going to tell you. They're eleven and fourteen. Oh god, and her husband. That poor man. Those poor girls.'

I put down the phone. I had two sisters. My mother's plane had crashed on take-off.

People talk about shock as mind numbing. But an image of a burning aircraft came to me. The smoke that filled the sky was indistinguishable from the fog, as acrid as burning coal.

I think of loss like the weight of a soul. When you dissolve loss into loss, nothing changes. Colour, texture, smell, everything remains the same. There is nothing to feel. No sadness, no grief. Everything is a mirage.

At Bethany, the maternity home where I was born, they took the babies from their single mothers right away. Before their mothers laid eyes on them. Before they understood they could see love made flesh in their child's eyes. Before they could make a fuss. Or scream down the ward. Although I'm told they often did both as they tried to find their missing babies.

Had my mother died on the day I was born they would have swaddled me in sadness, a child of sorrow and loss. Comforted by shared grief. But stranger adoption denies you that grief. One set of arms is considered as good as another. To the baby, there is no such distinction. To me, my mother died on the day I was born. She came alive again for three short days — phone call to phone call. And then she died again. The opposite of Easter.

But even at that point, grief was denied me. I was not one of those 'poor girls'. I'd never met her, after all. I had no right to my racing heart or the black-filled sky. There was no acceptable place to take my grief. We were strangers created out of stranger adoption.

I fed Ruth and sat her on a towel in the bathroom. The older girls stood with their backs to the wall, as if lined up for a photo, and watched as I undressed. We hold grief in our lungs. I found I could not breathe. My skin was on fire, and all I wanted was water. I stood under a cold shower. Rachel pulled aside the curtain, her face all concern, then she began to cry.

I dressed and hugged her, and we sat on the bed. Bonnie and Rachel took Ruth's hands and the three of them jumped. Their laughter caught me and I lay down. It was all the invitation they needed. Rachel burrowed under my arm. Bonnie tried to make the mattress bounce higher. Ruth scaled my hip, her arms aloft, before giggling and falling next to me.

I turned on the radio but missed the news and got the weather report. *Showers, briefly heavy in the morning, becoming isolated afternoon and gradually clearing.* Gradually clearing. Everything gradually clears.

'Let's go out for dinner,' I said. 'A special treat.'

They had never been to a restaurant and ran circles with excitement. I watched them dress themselves, fighting over a singlet and the hairbrush.

At the reception desk, the motel woman was reading a newspaper. I asked if there was anything about a plane crash. She shook her head, then remembered. 'On the radio. In Spain. Something about fog. Lots of survivors though.' She looked at her watch and turned on the radio. The beeps for the news sounded.

Two Spanish jetliners collided in heavy fog on a take-off runway here this morning, killing about 90 people and injuring more than 30 of the approximately 45 survivors.[7]

Jeannie was wrong. Surely my mother would have survived. But I knew she was dead. Something had changed. The lulling of a violin string in the moments after the note dies away.

Our bodies are echo chambers. We know things that make no sense. Today the science says we leave tiny pieces of ourselves in each other. Microchimeric cells slip across the placenta during pregnancy. In Greek mythology, a chimera is a shape-shifting creature. Fetal microchimeric cells left in the mother can migrate through her blood. In rat models, they have been seen to change shape as they rush to assist in healing a mother's injured heart.

None of us is as singular or autonomous as we like to think. My mother had held a filament of me within her body. And now even that tenuous thread was broken.

Today I am comforted and wowed by the science. But back then all I felt was the weight of knowledge. I had wanted this one thing so badly, I had caused a catastrophe.

Mavis calibrated her goodness through phrases and sayings. Uncomfortable questions always elicited the same response: 'Never trouble trouble till trouble troubles you, for you'll only trouble trouble and trouble others too.'

I was always the one who troubled trouble. An actor who breaks through the fourth wall and speaks directly to the camera. I had dared to step out of my assigned role. I had sought Pamela out and now she was dead. I had taken my broken-heartedness and passed it on to others. 'Those poor girls.'

I stared at the motel woman. 'Is it worse to lose all hope or never to have had it in the first place?' I thought I saw a tear forming in her dry eyes.

She frowned. 'Your children are hungry,' she replied.

'I'm on the other side of hope,' I said, but she had already turned away.

The almost-Italian restaurant was a short walk. Red-checked cloths covered the tables and they served chips with everything. There was a high chair for Ruth and I explained to the girls how to order from a menu. My heart's desire had grown so vast and fast, its destruction was now too much to contemplate.

I focused on my breathing, on the girls' chatter, on the drawings they did on the paper the waiter provided. The meal arrived — chips and fish for the girls and a plate of pasta for me. I wondered if they ate pasta in Spain. Who would cook for those poor girls? For them, it was the worst thing that could happen. But for me, it was nothing more than the opening and closing of desire. I cut the girls' fish into tiny bits and let them use their fingers.

I'd been living on hope for all my life. Consuming it like air. Brittle, shallow, stupid hope. Now we would have to go back. To the cold cottage and the insatiable chickens. To the peeling paint, the rusted bath, the curling lino and the boggy lawn. And the bush that grew back, reclaiming its true nature the minute I turned away.

I would start again. Because how you start is the most important thing.

Ruth knocked over the dish of tomato sauce, the red spraying like blood across the table. I wiped up the mess and smiled at my girls and we settled into silence, devouring our food as if we'd always been hungry.

9

You
are
an
electromagnetic
field

*The heart has its reasons which reason knows
nothing of . . . We know the truth not only by the
reason but by the heart.* — Blaise Pascal[8]

We drove home the next day, through Arthur's Pass,
over the mountain and into a storm. Gale-force winds
whipped at the car. I felt my mother's presence. As if she
were sitting beside me, holding the wheel steady, ensuring
I would not veer left to plunge over the gorge. I imagined
the vehicle sailing high for a moment, silent in the rain. The
children too surprised to scream. The long tumble as the car
disappeared, curtained from the road and devoured by the
bush. And there we would remain, nestled in trees too dense
to give up their secret.

When we came out onto the grassy flats, the sun
appeared. You cannot underestimate the miracle of sun in a
place that rains all the time. We were safe, and my mother's
spirit disappeared.

Bruce was not home. The chickens were loose and
came running toward us. The goat was gone. It was almost
Christmas but the house was damp and cold. The fire in the
wood burner had gone out. Apart from a few weeks during
mid-summer, we kept it ticking over. Warming the bones of
the house, Bruce had said as the wind whistled through the
window frames.

He came home a few hours later, a little drunk, which
was unusual for him. Jeannie had called him first. He'd
known about my mother's death before I did.

'I'm sorry,' he said, and held me for a moment. 'We
should pray about it.'

I stood stiffly while he intoned the magic words.
Tomorrow I would go to the welfare office and find out what
benefits a single mother of three could expect.

In my rational mind, I am agnostic. But imagination

escapes such limits. The visions began that evening as I slid into the bath. Although her face was a smudge, I was sure the woman in the car was my mother. They arrived at an airport. She applied red lipstick without a mirror. As she strode across the car park, the idle luggage boys blew into their chilled hands. Their pushcarts were no more than disembodied shapes in the fog.

I was in a trance in Runanga, topping up the bath with the last of the hot water. At the same time, I was shadowing the misty woman in Madrid.

I followed her into the terminal and waited beside her in line at the check-in counter. When it was her turn, the attendant spoke to a supervisor. There was no sound, but it was clear there was confusion over her seat. My mother took a fax from her bag, pointing to her reservation. The attendant inclined her head towards a group of Japanese couples. My mother smiled and they waved at her. Later I learned they were honeymooners on the first leg of their long flights home.

She stood in a queue at the glass doors to the tarmac. The fog blotted out the view. She was nervous, radiating a tension I could feel in my bathwater.

An overweight man in front dropped his tickets. He wore a camel-hair coat, the remnant of an elegance long since consumed. My mother helped him as the passengers behind shuffled in frustration. When the doors opened, they pushed through, out onto the milky tarmac to the plane. She pulled her jacket tight against the damp. Her clothes were too light. She had dressed for a New Zealand summer. She followed the large man up the stairs. He shuffled sideways down the aisle, the strap of his bag hidden in a furrow across his shoulder. The fog seemed to have followed them on board, glazing the cabin with apprehension.

She glanced at her ticket, unused to sitting in the middle of the plane. The man lowered himself into the embrace of his seat with a knowing smile. They were sitting together. The doors closed and the plane began to taxi.

'Mind if I lift the armrest?' The sound barrier had disappeared. His voice was syrupy and oddly fragrant, and it occurred to me that he was God. Or perhaps an angel, an oversize cherubim sent to escort her.

I was afraid to move, to even ripple the water in case the gap in time closed up. Desperate to know and terrified at the same time.

My mother lifted the armrest and looked out to the shrouded runway. The man leaned across, his arm doughy against her.

'Dense fog,' he said, and I could smell chocolate.

I heard the thunder of engines. Another aeroplane with its flashing lights split the fog. The fuselage was close enough to touch. The mist surrounded them, billowing like smoke, as it dissolved the edges of the man's coat.

The hot water ran out and the bath was cold. I got out, my head pounding. Bruce was asleep on the couch. I gazed out the window at the trees thick with new summer leaves and saw a child waving her arms. She stood on an observation deck and pointed to a patch of blue above the hulk of the dismembered plane.

Two weeks later I found a copy of *Time* magazine open on a table at our local pizzeria. Someone had turned the pages back to an article on a plane crash in Madrid. One photograph showed the ribs of the fuselage flat on its belly. In another four men carried the corners of a plaid blanket. They leaned away from the sagging weight of their cargo and there was no rush in their step.

I had seen it all from my bath and now here it was, my dream made real in a random magazine on a café table.

Does adoption cause a vivid imagination? Filling the gap between the known and unknown with fantasy?

W hen you grow up in a vacuum without transparency or truth, fabrication is your only refuge. As a child, I invented stories about my mother. She was famous, of course. A musician, a painter, a scientist. She was every passing thing I ever wanted to be.

But then I'd found her and made a terrible mistake by writing to her. My letter had caused her death.

So instead I began to write about the life I imagined *she* had. I invented her lovers and friends. I described her elegant home with crown mouldings and tall windows and deep carpets. I gave her a golden Labrador called Otto and a troubled teenage daughter who planned to run away. Her dissatisfied husband slept on the sofa, dreaming of lingerie and a secret life he kept from her. There was even a declawed kitten that lived behind her curtains.

Over the years, the stories changed. When I had a relationship with a disingenuous writer, I processed the fallout as if it had happened to my mother. When it was over, he sent me a file of letters he'd written, one or more a day for all the months. They began with pleasure. I was the shiny new thing in his life. I was better than his wife. I was all the mysteries rolled into one. Soon enough my contradictions were my downfall. By the end, he had transformed me into his own shadow self and I became every love who had failed him.

As I read his wounding words, I pretended he was my mother's lover, not mine. Because this is one of the things a mother does. She absorbs the blows for her child. Not all of them, and not forever. But she is there for her child of any age. When your children are small, protecting them is your overriding obsession. As mine grew up, I understood that this natural response does not change. Their danger is always my danger. Any threat to them is a threat to me.

It took a long time to realise that Mavis appeared to have no such capacity. Her parenting was competent and practical. Food, water, clothing, shelter. The mysterious and strange works of the heart were missing in our relationship. Were they unknown to her? Or was it inappropriate to share them with a stranger child?

But what if all Mavis wanted was the child she could not have, the one her heart *could* recognise? Perhaps she was undone by the failure of language to encompass the complexities of her inner world.

The Welsh understand. They call it *hiraeth*, a concept of deep homesickness. *Hiraeth* is more profound than just missing something. It is the unrequited hope that produces ever more unanswered longing. Welsh writer Val Bethell describes hiraeth as the language of the soul, the call from the inner self. 'Half-forgotten — fraction remembered.'[9]

There is a painting that has long fascinated me. By José Ferraz de Almeida Júnior (1850–1899), *Saudade* shows a dark-haired woman leaning against a window. There is a tear on the side of her nose, and she is reading a letter while holding her shawl over her mouth. The painting conveys dejection and longing in every molecule of her being. I had always thought the title was the woman's name. But then I discovered *saudade* is the Portuguese word for something beyond longing. There is no other word quite like it. They say it is the seventh most difficult word to translate. It describes a melancholic feeling of incompleteness, a desire for something absent that is being missed; a mysterious, transcendent and intimate mood caused by deep longing.

Was this what my past lover, the errant writer, was expressing as he filled the pages with my failings? Is this what my adopting mother was unable to communicate, even in the diligence of her caring?

The heart is the first organ that forms in the body. There is a divine symbiotic communication between the heart of the mother and that of her child. The Mexican scientist

Maria Teresa Sotelo understands all this. She says the mother–child connection is far deeper than we've imagined. 'The heart of the child can translate her mother's emotions. She knows if she is loved or not.' Sotelo describes pregnancy, birth and lactation as a process of molecular and cellular communication in the middle of an electromagnetic field. 'The baby's heart incorporates the heartbeat of the mother into its own heartbeat,' she says.[10]

Understanding these things, I am sad for Mavis. For me, everything is in service to that longing for connection, to *saudade*. It is a longing that pays no heed to mortal realities. I am almost sixty and still I ache for that one thing my agnostic mind reaches for but cannot quite grasp: the sound of my mother's heart beating within my own.

10

Abraham and Isaac went up a hill

We resumed our lives in Runanga as if I'd never been to Christchurch. I wanted Bruce to get a real job, a career. In reality, I wanted one myself but could not imagine what I could do or be.

Mavis had taken me to a careers adviser not long before I left home. They chatted as though I was not in the room.

'Well yes,' Mavis had said, 'she loves to write, but her spelling is atrocious.' She lowered her voice. 'She wants to go into radio.'

The careers adviser ignored me. 'It's tough to get into radio school. You mentioned she loves horses? Farming would be a good choice. She could marry a farmer.'

We were not radio school or university people. Ideas above your station, Max said when I dared to mention it.

Now a job came up at the Runanga council. Dog-catcher. It came with a bicycle, a rope with the ends wrapped in tape, and bite-sized packages of mince. I collected the packages from the butcher and carried them in a saddlebag as I rode around in the pre-dawn calm, eyes peeled for strays. The dogs of Runanga were an unruly lot. They delighted in enticing me down long winding driveways or up into the bush. Payment was by the dog and I was not particularly successful. But to be alone after years of babies clinging to every part of me was a relief. I loved that job and they gave me a great reference.

'Why don't you go to teachers' training college?' I suggested to Bruce one morning when I came in from biking all over the town. He was making porridge and the girls were still in their pyjamas. He nodded and said nothing, and I wrote away for the application form.

Jeannie called with an address north of Wellington and a phone number. Pamela's father Fred and Betty, his second wife. 'They'd like to hear from you,' she said. 'But be gentle, he's heartbroken at the loss of his daughter.'

I felt the familiar tug of unfairness. Pamela was his daughter and she was the mother of 'those poor girls', my half-sisters, and the wife of 'that poor man'. She did not belong to me in any way. I was an interloper. To know my mother was not a right. It was a favour.

I was beset with nerves. Apart from my girls, I'd not met a blood relative. I called and spoke to Betty.

'Come for a night,' she said. 'We have a spare room.'

The following week, I caught the bus from Greymouth to Picton. Ruth was still breastfeeding, so I took her along.

We boarded the ferry to Wellington. From the shore near Runanga, the sea smells of all the unmoored things that wash up. Dead fish, bloated seaweed, degrading plastic bottles. A rotted ham sandwich knotted inside a plastic bread bag. I held Ruth at the ferry railing, happy for the simple smells of salt and sun. A pod of dolphins joined us. They swam in mesmerising formation, the babies in the centre, surrounded by the adults.

In Wellington, we caught the train up the coast. The carriage was full of business types. There were women my age in smart skirts and jackets. I wore a cardigan I'd knitted myself. The pride I'd had in my tidy stitches disappeared.

Betty, a stout Scottish woman in a pleated wool skirt and a blouse buttoned tight, was waiting on the platform. My first impression was of a nun on day leave. I'd come all this way and had completely forgotten to bring a car seat for Ruth. We sat in the back seat while Betty spoke over her shoulder, explaining in detail how to grow a bumper crop of tomatoes.

'Fred's not himself,' she said when we pulled up outside their small Summit stone unit. 'You go in first.'

I knocked, and he opened the door right away. A tall thin man, he tilted forward, a stalk in the wind. I wanted to reach out and steady him. He peered at me and began to cry. I'd never seen a man cry before. At first, they were quiet tears sliding down his cheeks. Then he sat in a worn La-Z-Boy and put his head in his hands and wept.

Betty patted his back. 'Cup of tea, dear, coming up,' she said.

In the kitchen, she got out some pots and pans for Ruth to play with.

'Don't worry,' she said, 'it's you looking so much like her. And the baby. He gets a little confused. I imagine he thought it was her coming home with you.' She gazed out her kitchen window to the glasshouse where fat tomatoes hung on wilted vines. 'He regrets everything, you know. Lost it all.'

I took him his tea. He gulped at it and pointed to an old photo album beside the chair. We'd still not spoken. I opened the album. There were photos of my sisters with their ponies and pet dogs. In one they were in swimsuits at a competition watched over by the King and Queen of Spain. There was a trip to Thailand with tame snakes draped over their shoulders. I could see the echo of my children in their faces. But their lives were nothing like ours. There were snaps of a house with floor-to-ceiling curtains and a maid in the background. And there was my mother, a blanket over her knees, as she surveyed the views from a gondola in Venice. Her life after the false start of me.

I could not see myself in her.

Fred put his fingers to my face. I thought he would cry again, but instead he began to speak in a musical voice full of regret and pain. His accent was pure Manchester.

He condensed the facts into a simple story. After the war and incarceration in a Japanese prisoner-of-war camp, he'd become a painter and paperhanger. A New Zealand government-approved skill that got his family a ship's passage and a house in the new suburb of Tawa. 'A fresh start,' he said, then looked away. 'Ian, your uncle, hated it out here. He turned around and went right back.'

I tried to imagine my teenage mother on the ship, arriving from London into the deep green isolation of Wellington in 1959. She was already in her unthinkable 'state'.

He took out another album and pointed to a photo of Jessie, my grandmother, taken in a London pub. 'Dressed to the nines, she was, that night,' he said. There were photos of Pamela as a child in a garden surrounded by brick-edged lawns. In another, she was a young teenager standing next to Ian, her older brother, on the marble steps of a grand building. There was a picture of their house in Tawa, the bush-clad hills close enough to touch. Her life before me.

I understood I had divided them. Before me, they were an average family. I was the antapex, the point from which the solar system of their lives was always moving away. After me, Jessie died. After me, Pamela stopped speaking to her father. And now, on her way to meet me and to see him, she was dead and there would be no redemption.

There is a generally accepted narrative around adoption. It might be difficult, but everyone gets over it. The problem disappears and everyone moves on with their lives. In that fairytale, there is no loss. The family preserves its dignity. The young woman sacrifices her child to avoid the ruination of an out-of-wedlock baby. The stigma of illegitimacy disappears and everyone moves on with their lives. To allow others to take your baby is a courageous and loving thing to do.

It is this rhetoric of love that most disturbs me. We've whitewashed stranger adoption for so long we've blanched the emotion from it. We're told over and over that there is no greater love than to sacrifice your child for the greater good.

I've always wondered about the biblical story of Abraham

and his son, Isaac. It is echoed in the Muslim festival Eid al-Adha. The trusting boy accompanies his father on a walk up a mountain. Isaac asks his father, 'Hey, Dad, where's the lamb for the burnt offering?' Abraham ignores him. He's busy listening to the voice in his head that has told him to build an altar. He takes the wood that little Isaac has helped him carry. Perhaps Isaac was playing or watching the birds as Abraham sharpened his knife. Did he squirm and beg for his life as his father tied him to the makeshift altar? Did his mind collapse with the knowledge his father was about to murder him?

And we are told that this is love. That such a sacrifice will bring blessings more numerous than stars. We ignore the father's sadism, justified by his belief in God. Instead we focus on God's flip-flop that avoids the human sacrifice. We come away from this story relieved the child is saved, and with our belief that sacrifice is righteous and necessary to satiate the gods intact.

My grandfather had thrust his daughter and unborn grandchild into the night. In a new country. As if that act alone would appease the gods of gossip and shame.

I imagine my mother in her room in the house in Tawa. Secluded behind the net curtains as though marooned on a dinghy out at sea. Did her stomach churn, rising sour into her throat, as she waited for him to discover her sin?

I asked Fred how pregnant my mother had been.

'Enough to see,' he said, without looking at me.

Jessie must have known. Did she help her daughter to hide her state, only to allow her husband to lock the door behind her? Did Isaac's mother know that morning as she dressed her boy that her husband planned to murder him? I wondered then if my arrival had hastened Jessie's illness, the knowledge of what her husband would make her do exploding through her cells until they overwhelmed her body.

I sat with my grandfather in their small living room with its shelves of cheap ornaments. In the kitchen, Ruth continued to bang on the pots. It did not seem to occur to Fred that she was his great-granddaughter.

'My pretty ponies,' he said without looking up, his eyes red from crying. 'I used to call them my pretty ponies.'

He had been working at Kirkcaldie & Stains, the fancy department store, painting the walls in time for the grand opening of the 'off the peg' floor. Jess and Pammie. They came to visit him at work. He told me how proud he was to escort them through the revolving doors. 'Jessie was not too happy with the naked mannequins, I can tell you that.' He smiled at the memory. He recounted introducing them to his workmates, telling one lad to keep his eyes to himself. 'I thought she could get a job, a counter girl.'

I could have listened to him all night. But Ruth started to cry and I took her to the guest room. Twin beds pushed against the walls. She was always a contented baby, but I could not settle her. She took long ragged breaths, rigid with fury one minute, floppy with exhaustion the next. I held her damp heaving body tight, and it was as if she'd taken all the sadness of that house into her tiny limbs.

11

Husband, father, painter, paperhanger

We stayed one night. Ruth cried and fussed through the long hours. By morning we were both exhausted.

Fred said he slept well. 'Not a peep,' Betty said when I asked her about the noise. She smiled over her shoulder as she made porridge the old-fashioned way, with salt and butter.

After breakfast, Fred showed us the garden. He walked a wide margin around the glasshouse with the tomatoes. Dahlias were his thing. They lined the back fence, their drooping red and pink heads nodding in the sun. He touched each bloom as we walked by.

Betty watched us from the kitchen window.

'Tell you the truth —' Fred nodded towards her — 'can't stand them tomatoes. She grows them to spite me. But dahlias. Did you know you leave them in the ground over winter? They need a lot of mulch, mind.'

It occurred to me his head appeared large because his body had shrunk, his chest hollow, his arms all bone. 'Are you unwell?' I asked, and felt breathless from the intimacy of the question.

'No more than the next man.' He tapped the side of his head. 'And a bit funny up here sometimes.'

We sat on a garden seat behind the glasshouse hidden from the kitchen window, and I asked what he meant.

'Nonsense in me head.' He leaned towards me. 'The Japs.' His eyes welled up. There was a saucer of old rollie butts on the ground and he pushed it under the bench with his heel. I looked at his long thin fingers and could not help myself from stroking them. His hand quivered beneath mine. The sun reflected off the glasshouse. He told me about the brutal and arbitrary torture in the POW camp and the nightmares that haunted him. 'Filthy rice, a bit of grass stew.' He tapped his hollowed stomach. 'Dysentery, malaria. Still got an ulcer. Could never put on fat again.'

He unhooked a barometer from the fence behind us. 'Do

you have one of these?' he asked. When I said no, he explained how important it was to predict the weather. 'Especially for dahlias,' he said. 'They hate the frost. Take it. It's yours.'

The glass face showed all the options: Stormy, Rain, Change, Fair and Very Dry. 'Do you follow the weather?' I asked.

'Your grandmother —' He stopped and corrected himself. 'No, your great-grandmother, my mother Harriet. She loved a good storm. Would sit out on the step in all weathers just watching the sky. "I'm talking with the heavens, son," she would say. Tiny, she was, drunk, most of the time. But she could spin a yarn so you'd laugh at your own tears.' She died of a broken neck, falling down the stairs of her row house.

Betty came out with a cup of tea and a biscuit for us both. Ruth had been crawling around the lawn. Betty picked her up and took her into the house.

Fred watched her go. 'Good woman. A bit strict. I met her on the ship, taking my Jessie's ashes home.' He continued to talk as if time was running out, jumbling the timelines of his life. But when we got to Pam, my mother, his daughter, he stopped.

'Ask her.' He nodded towards the house. 'I told her everything.'

He said it still surprised him how many different people we are in our lives. 'I was a lad before the war. Then in the POW camp, thin as a shadow. Then a husband and father, a painter and paperhanger. Now? Nothing.'

It was a strange feeling to have such an intimate conversation with an elderly man I did not know. There was something between us. A sense of connection, an expectation of understanding. I had never spoken with Max like this.

Fred asked me about my favourite colour and nodded his approval when I told him. 'I've painted a lot of white walls,' he said. 'Good references, too. I'll show them to you.'

He staggered a little as we stood, and I realised he was more frail than he had let on. I held his arm as we went back into the house. And for a moment it felt like he was holding me up, that without him I would fall through the cracks. Without his story, I would not exist.

Until very recently, we assumed all inheritance was genetic and cultural. Nature and nurture. But now psychologists believe trauma is also inheritable. And scientists agree. Epigenetics shows how trauma alters cortisol levels in inheritable genes.

Dora Costa from the University of California investigated the lives of Civil War soldiers. They'd returned from Confederate prisoner-of-war camps like 'walking skeletons'. Costa extended her studies to their descendants. She found their health and life expectancy far below that of the general population, and she could show how inherited trauma affected their lives.[11]

In Australia, a study of 'Historical Trauma and Aboriginal Healing' explored the impact of hidden collective memory. Even non-remembered trauma is transmitted from generation to generation. The authors go as far as to describe historical trauma as a disease in itself.

Inherited trauma makes sense to me. We know that post-natal separation from the biological mother disrupts natural evolution. Nancy Verrier, who wrote a seminal book about adoption, *The Primal Wound*, describes how the experience of abandonment and loss is indelibly imprinted upon the unconscious mind.

In South Africa ancestor-worshipping Zulus regularly appease their dead. Constellation therapists believe every family has a collective conscience going back generations.

They say that by confronting our larger family stories, we can be freed from the pain we shoulder for our ancestors.

I grew up without ancestors and yet I carry my history unconsciously. Is it in my bone marrow? Or hovering above in my etheric being? Or perhaps in some undiscovered internal solar system? I worry I've passed the trauma to my children and grandchildren. And I fear that we still think babies are interchangeable. Or that each of us is born into a vacuum, with need of little more than care and feeding and a hug before bed.

Betty made lunch. We sat around the table and Fred talked about family. He described Pam's house near the whitewashed Moorish town of Mojácar. He'd visited her there two years before. Pam's husband had won it in a card game and they'd turned it into a resort with a golf course and an airstrip.

'He was terribly impressed with all that,' Betty said as I helped her with the dishes. She took a photo of my mother from her pocket. A young woman, maybe thirty, slim and stylish, looking directly at the camera. Looking at me. 'He wants you to have this,' she said.

'Did he force her to give me up?' I had to ask.

'Jessie was dying. He's too scared to ask about your life. In case, well, you know. He knew it was a mistake and he never stopped worrying about you.'

In the living room, Fred had let Ruth climb onto his knee and was playing a counting game with her fingers. I knelt beside him. 'I had a good life,' I said. 'You have nothing to worry about.'

He glanced at me and tears filled his eyes again. 'Did they treat you well?' he asked.

I smiled. 'They gave me everything they could.'

Fred put Ruth down and struggled from his chair. He

took down a VHS tape and pulled the curtains. I had thought it might be a home movie with Pamela. Instead it was a promotional video for a luxury resort called Cortijo Grande.

'I forgot I had this,' he said as the grainy 1970s film began. Pamela had owned far more than a house. It was an entire development over hundreds of acres above the Mediterranean. There were villas and bars and swimming pools. She did all this. She'd had an idea and grown it into a wonderland in the mauve hills of southern Spain. I watched in silence, overcome by the smallness of my life, the failure of my curiosity and imagination.

When it was over, Fred stared at the television. 'Is she really dead?' he asked.

Betty put her hand on his shoulder. He looked at me and up at her. 'That's not her, is it?'

Betty took his hand. 'Time to go.'

She decided we would take a drive past the old house in Tawa on the way to the railway station. As we got closer, Fred began to breathe heavily. His head dropped forward for a moment. Then he waved his arms as if hitting at unseen bugs. Ruth started to cry. Betty pulled over. She indicated that we should get out. As Fred fiddled to undo his seat belt, she locked the car, trapping him inside.

'He's having a turn,' she said. 'Can you knock on a door and get someone to call you a taxi?'

Fred pressed his face against the window, his eyes glazed. He pounded on the glass, screaming at us to get away, to leave him alone, to let him out.

Betty dabbed at her eyes. 'He gets violent,' she said. 'Thinks he's back in the prisoner-of-war camp.' She showed me a bruise on her arm, another the shape of a shoe on her leg. 'He was always gentle. He doesn't mean it. He thinks I'm a guard in the camp. He tries to escape, to get away from me.'

It had started a few months before when she woke one

night to find him gone. The police brought him back an hour later, his pyjamas muddy, his eyes still wild with confusion.

'An ambulance,' I suggested. Betty shook her head. 'He'll calm down soon. I'll call his doctor when we get home, he'll give him a sedative. It always works.'

A woman came out of a house and asked if we needed help. Fred was still yelling, banging his fists on the console and the roof of the car. I caught a few words: Jap bastards, mongrels. 'I've called the police,' the woman said. 'I didn't know what else to do. I thought the baby might get hurt.'

The police arrived and Betty placed her hand on the window. 'I'm sorry, I'm sorry,' she said to Fred as he continued to scream obscenities.

Betty explained to the policeman that her husband needed a doctor. She asked him to retrieve my suitcase from the boot. She called me his granddaughter, and asked if they could drive me and Ruth to the railway station.

I waited with her until the medics arrived. He'd calmed down by then. When they opened the door, he dropped his head and let them help him out and into the ambulance. He hunched his shoulders, his eyes glazed as if he did not recognise us.

Betty reassured me he would be fine. They'd forgotten his pills with all the excitement. And the lack of sleep. She hugged me and told me he loved me.

'Will you tell me more about what happened when I was born?' I asked. She agreed to write, and drove off, following the ambulance.

My grandfather, Frederick William Sumner, died in a locked ward at the psychiatric hospital a few months after I met him. 'Nothing wrong with him,' Betty told me later. 'He just turned his face to the wall and willed himself to die.'

12
Wondering where the lions are

Walking into Wellington Railway Station, I felt as if I'd arrived in another country. People moved with purpose beneath vaulted ceilings. Without a glance, they strode over the large compass tiled into the floor. I stood to one side and watched them, longing to be part of all that forward motion.

I called Mavis and Max from a phone box. Mavis's voice was full of surprise.

'I'll get Dad,' she said. We'd never had a conversation without his presence. On the phone, he would pick up the extension. There were no shared intimacies unless he was part of it. No mother–daughter secrets. We'd never once been for lunch or shopping or any outing that did not involve the two of them.

I kept the conversation short. I was in Wellington to meet someone and could I stay the night?

It was rush hour on the train to Upper Hutt. The wind came up, flinging the sea over the tracks that ran along the margin of the harbour. Fresh rain pitted the surface of the water. I wondered if Fred had gone home, or if they'd kept him in hospital. I thought of the sun-drenched images from the VHS. I wanted to walk the pathways above that calm and distant sea. I longed for arid hills. For a dry and sapless heat to smother the damp.

We waited as Upper Hutt Station emptied of people. The car park was soon deserted. Late sun crept across the litter and oil stains. I had no idea how I would explain things to them.

It was not that I had no right to find my family, it was that they did not recognise I had one. My desires did not exist because there was no framework for them to exist within.

I needed to put Ruth down and stretch my body. Mavis and Max arrived late. He always drove. He had allowed her only recently to get her licence. 'Cricket?' I asked. I knew from experience they were late because he'd been listening to cricket on the radio. He could not miss a second. Mavis inclined her head. An acknowledgement and a warning.

We drove without speaking to their stucco home at the end of a cul-de-sac in the middle of a seventies subdivision. The air pressure was dropping, the storm from Wellington circling Totara Park.

Mavis and Max did not ask questions. If they were curious about anything, they kept it between them. They were waiting for me to explain why I'd come. 'If she wants to tell us, she'll tell us,' was one of Mavis's sayings. I look back, amazed at how everything controversial was off-limits. We did not debate in our family. We did not disagree or argue a point. And most of all we did not contradict Max.

Mavis made dinner. As always she refused my offer of help. Max grumbled as she sent him to get the battered high chair from the garage.

In the living room, I sat on the floor in front of the console that held the record player. My old records were still here, and I pulled out Bruce Cockburn's album *Dancing in the Dragon's Jaws* and put it on. Ruth clapped and I turned it up for his song 'Wondering Where the Lions Are'.

The song consumed me in inexplicable grief. I shut my eyes and lifted my small daughter and danced with her.

Max came in and turned it off. The silence felt like the last moments under the bath water, balanced on the edge of a different eternity. 'Set the table,' he said. 'You're not a teenager anymore.'

I laid out the cutlery and sat down to feed Ruth. Breastfeeding made them uncomfortable.

'Does she eat real food yet?' Mavis asked.

Did I read too much into her comment? In their home, I was as sensitive as the millibars of the barometer nestled in my suitcase. I wondered if it had picked up the weight of the squall pressing down on us.

Mavis served, and we took our places at the table and began to eat.

'I've been at my grandfather's house,' I said. They looked at each other and returned to their chops and mashed potatoes.

The Earth rotates from west to east, dragging the atmosphere with it. Birds fly away from low-pressure systems as if they know a change is coming. All I felt was a wind of fury. I wanted to be in the eye of a storm. I wanted the shock of thunder, the burn of lightning. I wanted to hurt them. But most of all, I wanted them to respond, to engage in a real way. But we continued to eat, like an ordinary family, no different from any other.

'Did you hear about the plane crash in Madrid a few weeks ago?'

Max nodded and mentioned the fog and pilot error. This was an acceptable topic for conversation.

I took a deep breath. 'My mother was on that plane.' A polar wind wrapped itself around us. 'She was on her way here, to New Zealand. To meet me.'

Mavis let out a small, wounded sound. I took out the photo of Pamela that Betty had given me and held it up. Max placed his knife and fork on the table. He grabbed the photograph from my hand. He tore it in half and screwed it into a ball and threw it across the room.

'There is your mother.' He pointed to Mavis, his face red with anger.

Ruth began to cry, and I lifted her from the high chair and went to the spare bedroom. I pulled back the net curtains and opened the window onto the unpainted corrugated-iron fence. I wanted to leave. But there were no trains at night. I had no money for a taxi or a motel and all my energy was gone.

They usually stayed up late watching television. But tonight an old rugby match recorded on VHS boomed through the wall. I could hear Mavis washing the dishes.

When the house was quiet and Ruth was asleep, I tiptoed out to get a glass of water. Mavis was sitting in the dark. The crumpled photograph lay on the kitchen table. She had taped the two pieces together and had tried to smooth it out. I sat beside her and went to take her hand, but she pulled away.

'We will not speak of this again,' she whispered. 'We'll take you to the station in the morning.' Her voice was devoid of warmth.

My desire to know my family and to share that with them had made me clumsy, unmindful of their feelings. Deep in the heart of stranger adoption is an unspoken contract. You are acquired to resolve childlessness. You cannot be both the cure for infertility and someone else's child at the same time.

William Makepeace Thackeray said, 'Mother is the name for God on the lips and in the hearts of little children.'[12] By looking for my mother, I had failed to act as if I was born to my adopting parents. Over that meal, we were all undone by the failure and otherness of my blood. Nothing in me resembled them. I had named the elephant in the room. The spell cast at my birth was now broken.

I believe most adopted people experience this 'otherness'. Even those who declare the success of their pairing. Nancy Verrier talks about the fear of dying experienced by a baby taken from its mother. To assuage that fear, we become alert to the signs and symbols of how not to be the 'other'. We become mimics.

The French surrealist writer Caillois calls mimicry, or mimesis, a survival mechanism. It is the ability to turn into a copy of something else. Fitting in is a trick I carry with me. I had always thought of it as a sign of mastery. But Caillois says it indicates a lack of control. A type of subjugation to the dictates of the environment. He calls it spatial disorientation, a disturbance between personality and space.

Mimicry is not the same as belonging. We need deep ponds to contain the sediments of ancestry. All that primordial muck of inheritance. The stories of the drunks and saints and raconteurs are like the fossils of our forebears. Without them, our lives are as shallow as a puddle.

I have a love–hate relationship with family memoirs. All those detailed histories to draw on. The protagonists so often in flight from suffocating pasts, their resolutions found in return to the fold. But I had nothing to run from and no fold to return to.

Mavis and Max shared so little of themselves or their families. I knew the poverty of the West Coast of the South Island formed them. Their forebears were immigrants and settlers. Max's father died young in a hit and run, his mother was taken by an asthma attack. He grew up Catholic in a town divided by religion. Mavis's parents were farmers after the war. Their allocated land was so stony they walked away with nothing. She had wanted to stay at school but her father made her leave at fifteen. But even in writing these brief descriptions I feel like an intruder, with no right to connect their stories with mine.

There's a little darkness in every family. But family secrets are inheritance too. We hear them or intuit them, and they become ours to tell or keep as we see fit. I'll never know if Mavis and Max would have shared themselves with their own children.

When Max told his workmates they were planning to adopt, the men cautioned him. 'You don't know what you're getting,' is how Mavis later relayed the wisdom of the Railway Workshops of Invercargill. Was that one remembered comment enough to cause Max's relentless frost? His unconscious fear of the 'other'?

'But he made you a doll's house,' Mavis said when I once tried to broach his coldness with her. 'What more evidence of his love do you need?'

I had forgotten about the doll's house. There was a time when hobbies mattered. Max did paint-by-numbers. He painted a rocking horse. And assembled kitsets. I see him in the shed, late into the night, his dark hair slicked back as he bent to paint the tiny furniture. I wonder if he was making it for the other child? The invisible one whose shadow I carry, the one he might have had, the one I should have been. I loved that doll's house and played with it for years. By the time I had my own children, Mavis had given it away to another family. 'They love rugby,' she'd said when I asked why.

Being with my grandfather that day, I felt comfort in his Manchester accent. I could have held his hand forever. Sitting beside him, I'd felt strangely normal. I learned more about Fred, his remorse, his heart and his life in that one visit than in all the years with my adopting father. And then it occurred to me. There was another father out there, just as there was another mother.

The next morning I took my damaged photograph and started my journey back to Runanga. This is good, I thought. They've revealed their hand. I can absorb this blow because it is the lowest point of my life. We can only rise above ourselves now.

Ah, my foolish optimism. We never did speak of that night again.

13

How many times can you change your name?

With three small children, nothing ever goes to plan. It took months to wind up our joint affairs, to sell our house and move from Runanga to Christchurch. I'd stopped tending the garden and the lawns were already too long for the push mower. Vines were consuming the chicken coop. As we drove away it began to rain and I could hear the distant ocean sucking at the gravel beach.

We had fought over the stupid stuff. The girls' beds, the weaving loom he'd made me, the kitchen table. In his mind, it all belonged to him. My place in our family was through our children. By taking them away, I forfeited everything, including his financial support.

The Baptists came to his rescue. He forgave his parents their sins, and they took him back into the fold of family and religious support. They found him a manse on a sunny corner next to one of their empty churches. The world loves a single father. Especially after the devastation of a runaway wife. The Christian ladies brought him cooked meals and furnished his house. He started teachers' training soon after, so could only look after his children on weekends.

We moved into a concrete block of flats. One bedroom, a tiny kitchen and a toilet that leaked. I lugged second-hand mattresses up two floors. The previous tenant left behind a sofa and a coffee table with a cracked glass top.

We fell into a routine. I cared for the girls during the week. We walked everywhere and made friends at kindergarten. There was a beauty in our rhythms. We talk about the hardship of the single mother, but not the freedoms. I loved caring for my children alone. I felt my heart relax a little. When they are young, your children do not judge you. They look into your eyes and see only the good. We laughed a lot.

Bruce picked the girls up on Friday evenings. He'd kept the car as he needed it to get to training college. When they were gone, I would take a bath, my head above the water, my breath even. At around 10 p.m. I walked and bussed to my new job at a private musicians' club. We opened late and closed early. I ran the bar, serving drinks to wired musos till three in the morning. I walked home beneath the willows along the banks of the Avon River. The pre-dawn mist smothered the stink of cigarettes and beer that clung to my hair and clothes. Hunched inside my coat, I kept to the shadows, imploring the sun to rise above the horizon.

The separation caused another issue. My name.

My adopted name had always felt inauthentic. It was an ill-defined feeling that took years to comprehend. Barbara McG was perfectly serviceable. But even now, as I type, it makes me uncomfortable.

On marrying Bruce at eighteen I became Barbara White and was happy to be someone else for a time. But what name could I use now?

I waited till late on a Saturday and called home. Mavis answered. Max was in the garden. 'Do you happen to remember my name before you adopted me?' I asked.

'I'll get Max,' she replied. I heard the screen door bang and the tone of her raised voice but not the words. She came back on the line. 'They didn't tell us,' she said. 'I've already told you we know nothing. We got you and that was all that mattered.'

I made my voice soft and warm and thanked her for putting up with me. I did not want to fight.

'We talked to Bruce and the girls,' she said. I waited. It was unlikely she and Max would ask why I'd left him. But even if they did, I could not have explained the valley between us. 'He misses you so much,' Mavis said.

'He only has the girls on weekends.' It was impossible to hide my defensiveness. 'And he has plenty of support.'

Max coughed to let me know he was listening on the extension. I was straying into unwelcome territory.

'We have to go,' Mavis said, and they hung up.

I called Jeannie. She would know the name Pamela had given me. But Jeannie was unsure. I wanted to ask all the questions. Did Pamela talk about me in the weeks and months after? Did she use my name? Did she share her secrets?

'Come and meet me next time you're in Wellington,' Jeannie said. 'We'll talk then.'

I wrote another letter to the Department of Social Welfare. Trying again to find my files, to access any information on my identity. Weeks later, the same reply came back: 'We have no trace of you in our records.'

Months went by and there it was on the six o'clock news. An amendment to the Adoption Act 1955 had passed into law. Adopted people could now access a version of their original birth certificate.

I applied right away. Counselling was mandatory. I was twenty-five with three children, but my desire to know was insufficient. I had to prove to the counsellor I was mature enough to know my own identity.

She was a motherly older woman with a warm air of disapproval. 'Some things should remain hidden.' She glanced at the photos of happy families that covered one wall of her office. And I wondered if they were adoptions she had brokered. 'Be careful what you wish for,' she said as she signed my form with a tiny signature.

I imagined Pamela boarding the plane, the door closing behind her, the fog rolling in. The counsellor was right. And now there was nothing left to wish for.

I took the precious form to the Social Welfare office and went home to wait.

I've altered my name seven times. I used to change everything with regularity. Glasses, hairstyles, furniture, lovers, husbands and friends — everything was movable. I've burned through my life like a campfire of twigs. I've moved house thirty-four times. My restless journey was almost unconscious. I would once have described myself as peripatetic. The idea of not belonging was who I was. It was not so much that I'd lost my identity but that I'd never had one.

'Who am I?' may seem like a question at the core of being human. But social theorist Zygmunt Bauman calls it a postmodern issue. 'Identity as a concrete concept would hardly occur to any of us if it were not denied in some way . . . When "belonging" remains your fate — a condition with no alternative — identity does not occur to people.' He says that until quite recently the time and place of your birth determined your identity. Very few occasions arose for questioning provenance.

Bauman does not mention stranger adoption. He died before the current practice of buying and selling anonymous gametes. But his work describes the internal dislocation experienced by adopted people. And now that extends to those created in service to the fertility industry.

We are so reluctant to grapple with the idea that each of us intrinsically belongs somewhere. That humans are not interchangeable commodities. That eggs and sperm are not random raw ingredients. Being uplifted from your place in history and grafted onto the tree of strangers is a profound loss — to both the individual and the continuum of their genealogy. Trying to construct an identity in the face of that loss is difficult. Bauman says it's like assembling a jigsaw puzzle that has lost its box. 'With no image to consult, you may never know which pieces are missing.'[13]

I remember the plain brown envelope franked with the Department of Social Welfare logo. I took it to the bathroom and sat on the toilet seat. My name was Lilian Sumner. At that moment, I wanted to be her more than anything. An ethereal name without sharp edges, a name that conjured warmth.

Our names carry resonance and energy. In the esoteric world, onomancy is the divination of names. They say that the meaning, sounds and rhythms of the name you choose for your child make the tasks of that new soul easier. Names connect us to the past. They are genealogical roadmaps.

Barbara means stranger or traveller from a foreign land. There was once a Saint Barbara imprisoned in a tower by her father. He killed her for refusing to recant her beliefs and was later killed by a bolt of lightning.

Lilian means an offering or a vow. A name wrapped up in flowers, purity and beauty.

I started calling myself Lilian right away, but it did not go well. Bruce laughed. 'Everyone will think you're mental,' he said.

Max responded with silence. 'You have to understand,' Mavis said years later, after he'd passed away. 'He was an only child, the last of his line. His name was important to him.'

I asked why they'd had no problem with my married name.

'That's different,' she said. We were in her kitchen. She had a small portable document shredder on the bench. They'd begun to shred anything showing their names after a news item about how easy it was to steal someone's identity.

'Do you not see the irony?' I asked as she fed in a bank statement.

She frowned and looked away. 'This would be very good in your compost,' she said.

I left with a bag of shredded names, drove away and parked around the corner and laughed till I cried.

My history, my family, my mother and my name were erased. Mavis replaced my mother's name with hers on my birth certificate.

First names are more personal, a friend said. She felt I should soften the blow by changing my name gradually. Start with Sumner, she said. They won't be quite so antagonistic. So I went ahead and changed my surname by deed poll.

While I waited for my new identity, the police raided the bar at the musicians' club. The patrons scattered. A cop went to put me in handcuffs but thought better of it and held the door of the car. 'I'll drive you home,' he said. We stopped outside my flat and he took his time writing down my details. I gave him my new name. He asked if I knew we lacked a licence. I explained we'd recently moved from the West Coast. I was a single parent, working weekends to support my kids.

'It's a good defence,' he said.

When my court date arrived, I dressed the girls in their best clothes and we waited in a pew until they called my name. Barbara Sumner. I stood in the dock, and the judge looked at my girls and then at me. He read his notes and asked the same question. Did I know I was selling alcohol illegally? I shook my head and wiped a tear, and Rachel broke from the others and ran towards me.

The judge smiled. 'I understand,' he said. 'I apologise for putting you through this, Miss Sumner.' He discharged me without conviction.

As we left the courthouse, we passed the arresting officer. 'Nice performance,' he said, and slow-clapped me out the door.

14

A cosmological view of time

The musicians' club shut down and I was out of a job. Bruce came to pick up the girls. Our agreement no longer suited him.

'I need more time to myself,' he said. We were standing at the bottom of the concrete stairs to my flat. 'I can do the day and overnight on Saturday only.'

I was not in a placating mood. 'It's interesting,' I said, 'how resources and opportunity concentrate around the father.' Both of us were smiling to fool the girls we were still friends.

'You took away my children, so you took away my responsibility. Your choice.' We watched the girls in the car, fussing over their seat belts. 'By the way,' he said, 'I have a girlfriend. Can you return that bag of raw wool you took? She's learning to spin and weave.'

I'd left behind almost everything. The loom on which I'd made rugs to cover the cold floors, the spinning wheel and a half-knitted jersey.

'I hope she likes waterbeds,' I said.

'You'll never be a nice person,' he replied.

He brought the children back the next day. They reported his girlfriend had already moved in and was wearing a skirt I'd made. She had my sewing machine, too. I wondered what it would be like to step into another woman's shadow.

I went back to Piko Wholefoods where the same large man was waiting in line. He saw me and smiled. 'No foehn winds today?'

'We're in the Zone of Calms,' I replied, repeating the unusual weather report from the day of the motel. The day Jeannie called.

I was wary of men, but David exuded kindness. 'How about lunch?' he asked, and paid for my groceries. The older girls were at kindergarten. He squatted in front of Ruth in her stroller and laughed when she patted his bulging stomach.

We went for toasties at the bakery nearby. David was an actor's agent. He was warm and funny and generous. It felt like I knew him already.

And then I realised I'd seen him before. The vision I'd had in the bath in Runanga, the plane crash clear as day. He'd dropped his tickets and my mother picked them up. He'd shuffled on board and held her hand as his camel-hair coat dissolved in the heat. When I explained it to David, he smiled in the same syrupy way and did not question the madness of it.

The next time I saw him, he brought a photocopy of a *New York Times* article.

90 ARE KILLED AS JETLINERS COLLIDE ON MADRID RUNWAY IN HEAVY FOG

I learned how the smaller plane landed in the murk and missed a runway sign. It turned too soon and ploughed into the middle of the Iberia aeroplane, tearing it in half. A few survivors walked away with minor injuries. Much of the luggage remained intact. The fog was so thick a survivor running from the burning wreckage had to show rescuers where to go. Charred clothing and debris were everywhere. They covered the burned and mutilated bodies with blankets. Captain Carlos Lopez Barranco crawled from his damaged cockpit, shouting: 'The runway was mine!'

That summer in Christchurch, the days were sticky, the nights cool. I carried the article everywhere, feeling its presence in my pocket or bag. One Sunday we went to a concert in the park. We lay on the grass, the sky filled with mares' tails, those high, trailing cirrus clouds. The girls danced in front of the stage as the Topp Twins sang 'Untouchable Girls'. Ruth curled up beside me with a blanket over her face. She disliked loud noises and crowds. My vision wavered and I took a deep breath and closed my eyes.

It was not a hallucination exactly. More like an occulism with reality twisting away until the park became an airport. Two girls, young teens, stood on a viewing platform overlooking the runway. I knew without knowing they were my sisters. A man I assumed to be their father stood with them. The image was so clear I could see the younger one had smeared lipstick over the edges of her lips.

The air was soupy. Madrid expected dry cold in winter, not this damp seep. The father leaned over the railing towards the shape of an aeroplane in the fog. 'There.' He pointed to a disembodied hand pressed against the tiny round window near the front of the plane.

'That's not her,' the older girl said with disdain. The father put his arm around her. His voice rang clear in my ear. 'It'll be over soon, sweetie. Before you know it you'll be grown up. You won't even remember this day, let alone how awful it feels to be fourteen.'

She shrugged away and turned to the glass wall overlooking the terminal. The younger girl breathed a circle of condensation on the glass. She practised her signature, the last letter curling back through the others. The shadow of their mother's plane loomed in the reflection. It rose out of the fog, then disappeared as the engines roared and they taxied away.

'Can we go now?' the older girl asked.

The scream of an engine in reverse filled them. An explosion saturated the air. The sound permeated every cell in their bodies. The father dragged his girls under the flimsy protection of his coat. And then an infinite silence — before the glass wall shattered and fell onto the screaming people beneath.

For a moment, the fog parted like cut cloth to reveal a patch of blue above the dismembered plane. Father and daughters ran towards the stairs that led back into the terminal. Behind them, black smoke billowed across the tarmac and over the viewing platform.

Years later, I learned my sisters were at school that day. Their father was away. She was on her way to you, he wrote in a letter. He told me Pamela died on impact. The cataclysm was so great her necklace fused with her breastbone.

My sisters and their father were not there that day. And yet in my vision I'd seen it through their eyes. A doctor once told me I had false memory syndrome. For a while, I believed him. To qualify you need to think your real life is happening in another timeline of existence. And somehow you've slipped from it, into this other, less real world.

Many adopted people share the sense of living the wrong life. The possibility of another life exists in your marrow. But we cannot be in two places at once. There is no permeable wall between the past and the present. If there were, fact and truth would cease to exist. So was the dream of the crash a false memory, an aberration, or something else?

A few weeks after the hallucination at the park, we were at Sumner Beach. The sea had turned cold and the girls hunted for crabs along a stretch of rocks. I spread the blanket and put up an umbrella. The trance rolled in again so that I was standing on the tarmac, emergency vehicles all around. There was no sound except for the sea and the girls' laughter. But I was running with a group of medics towards the remains of the burning plane. Foam lay thick on the ground. An ambulance officer stumbled past, carrying an unconscious child. I put out my arms, and he passed him to me. I lay him on a sheet on the slick tarmac and brushed back his black curls to see his eyes wide open and empty.

The girls returned, piling onto the blanket, their sandy bodies warm from the sun. David arrived with buckets and spades and a bottle of wine. I told him everything. He listened and absorbed my stories of ghost worlds, of the taste of fog, gritty and acrid with smoke.

A while later, we were eating sandwiches in David's office. 'A friend will be joining us,' he said as a man in yellow leather boots walked in.

He shook my hand and looked at me with his head on one side as if deciding.

'Can I buy you new shoes?' I asked.

'You're clearly from the provinces,' he replied. 'Call me Hampster.' We made plans to meet on the weekend. 'We'll go shopping,' he said.

Be careful, David warned me. But I was heedless. Hampster was from another world. He made movies. He would talk endlessly about himself and catch it and smile. He asked questions that masqueraded as curiosity. A technique he'd perfected to avoid anything uncomfortable. He said he had recently left his wife. Only he hadn't. He said he lived in Auckland. Only he didn't. He ate at restaurants as though they were his natural habitat and made fun of my poor wine choices. He drove too fast and I let him, and it almost killed me.

15

Hear the cry for home

On the first date Hampster held the door of his red Porsche and I knew I was in trouble. We went shopping. He bought me a sweatshirt, shoes and a jacket, dressing me to suit his style. But he made me laugh and held my hand in private and let me drive his car. Of course, I was smitten. The accessories swayed me. I'd had so few of them, and for a while I mistook them for the real thing.

One night, in the silence of sleeping children, I took out a copy of *Metro* magazine. The first issue, from July 1981. I'd found it in a second-hand bookstore in Greymouth. Can a magazine change your perception of life? I read and reread an article about a suburb called Ponsonby. It was not Madrid. But they had cafés in Ponsonby. Auckland was warm, and Christchurch felt clogged with the past.

Hampster was erratic. He made a fanfare of everything, arriving with a flourish, leaving in a squeal of tyres. A 'big-noter' is how Max would have described him.

Mavis was still not speaking to me. But she would call Bruce to ask after the children. I phoned her one night. 'Everything's going well, Mum,' I said, pretending she'd asked. 'It's a bit of a struggle, though. The benefit hardly covers the basics.'

I could hear her smile down the phone. 'You've made your bed,' she said.

A while later, Hampster suggested I go with him to Auckland. We'd drive up and he'd pay my airfare back after a week. We set the date, and on Sunday morning I walked over to Bruce's house. We talked while the girls played in another room. Reluctantly he agreed to extend his childcare while I was away.

He drove us back towards the flat and began to berate me, angry that I'd derailed his life. 'If it were just you in the car, I'd drive us into the fucking river,' he said.

He never swore, and Bonnie leaned forward in her car

seat. 'It's okay, Daddy.' She patted his shoulder.

We were beside the Avon and he swerved from the road onto the grass. The ducks that huddled over the banks flew up around the car. 'I could do it,' he hissed.

Rachel began to cry. 'Ducks, Daddy, ducks,' she said.

He stopped, and I leaned over and took the keys and got out. 'Let's talk over here.' We unbuckled the children. His girlfriend, Alice, had made them sandwiches, and the girls ran down to the water to feed them to the ducks.

'We made this mess together.' I touched his hand.

He snatched it away. 'You're like a bird of prey. Without Alice in my life, I don't know what I'd do.'

I'd caught sight of Alice's blonde hair a couple of times. But she always disappeared when I arrived at his house and she refused to meet me.

He'd never been violent or even raised his voice. Our arguments and displeasures communicated in silences and pot-shots. Six years of playing our roles and this was our first real argument. The ducks surrounded the girls and we paused to watch them. They were too far away to hear the bitterness and recrimination.

'Don't speak to me ever again,' he said. 'Unless it's about the girls. Don't ask for money. I'll give you nothing. I don't care if you starve.'

'Shall we shake on that?' I asked, trying for levity.

'You've ruined me,' he replied, and I knew it was true.

The following week I was in the car with Hampster. The weather was grey and overcast. We sped along the Kaikōura coast, listening to Van Morrison. The sea grew dark, lidded with masses of cumulonimbus. On the ferry to Wellington, my stomach heaved with the waves. Standing at the railing in the freezing wind, I wanted to strip off all my clothes. I was desperate to be so in the moment that no other moment existed. I felt the rush and fear of the high diving board and the pull of the water, the yearning to plunge.

He came over and hooked his arm through mine. 'You're chilled through,' he said.

I shivered and pointed to the circles of light that surrounded the moon. 'That's an ice crystal halo. Ring around the moon means rain soon.'

We stayed in Hampster's house, hidden in the hills above Wellington. In the bathroom, and later when I looked in the bedside drawer, it was clear his wife had not left. I should have said something, taken the next ferry and a bus home. But I felt new with him. As if being twenty-five with three children was not old.

We visited a friend who'd arrived from Canada. We walked into the house and she was on a ladder, wallpapering the hall. They hugged and laughed and talked about the film business in Vancouver. Her pale curly hair fanned around her head. She breathed in the energy of the room and reflected it back and I felt like I was bathing in her light.

The next day we drove north towards Napier. Towering macrocarpas lined Highway 50. I still remember the exact spot, a sharp bend near Ongaonga. Hampster took it too fast and the car spun out. He laughed and put his foot down.

We rolled into Napier and I thought about visiting Mavis and Max. They'd recently moved there from Upper Hutt. Later I would think of their move as returning to the scene of the crime. We drove past their house. Max was in the driveway, washing his car. He turned at the sound of the Porsche, spraying water over the lawn. I raised my hand, but his face was devoid of recognition and we drove on. Perhaps he did not see me.

I tried to explain to Hampster how it felt not to belong anywhere.

'We'll find a motel.' He smiled. 'And I can be your Daddy.'
I thought again that it was time to go home to my kids.

We visited Mavis and Max the next morning. Max did
not mention he'd seen the car the previous day. We sat at
the table and drank tea and talked about the weather and
how their cat loved her new home. As we drove away, the
sun came out for the first time in days and I closed my eyes.
Hampster put Van Morrison on again.

We drove to Tauranga and stayed with his friends. I
was anxious to be away. I'd never been to Auckland.
I wanted to walk along Ponsonby Road and see if any of it
matched the image I'd conjured in my mind.

We took the twisting, steep road over the Kaimai Ranges.
As he was passing a truck, Hampster leaned forward to
change the CD and swerved into the path of an oncoming
car. I saw it bearing down on us and thought: My turn, my
poor girls. It hit my side, the Porsche collapsing around my
legs, spinning in silence.

When I came to, Hampster was sitting on the grass
nearby, his head in his hands. I noticed the jagged edges of
my teeth. Somewhere nearby a baby was crying. The car
lurched forward, sliding by degrees down the bank towards
the gorge. I could hear my girls laughing as they chased the
chickens.

As they cut me from the wreckage I woke to the shock
of blood over the new clothes and the agony of movement.
A fireman leaned over me, 'You're so lucky,' he said as they
pulled the stretcher up the bank over the wet bracken. I'm
told a truck driver tied a rope around the bumper to halt the
car's further descent into the gorge. The mother and her two
small children in the other vehicle survived with broken
bones. It was her baby I'd heard crying.

Later they said I was delirious, repeating a nonsensical sentence: The runway was mine, the runway was mine. I remember waking in the car, amazed at the beauty of the bush dense with green. And the water below sparkling in the sunlight, calling me in.

16

Oh
so
lucky

In the dream, I am sprawled across a sun-warmed boulder in the middle of a hidden river. The water is languid and deep. Birds swoop low as if checking on me. I slip into the water and drift in the lazy current as my body grows heavy. For a moment there is panic, a breathless struggle, and then a buoyant peace.

I woke to the weight of plaster on one foot, a thick bandage on the other. There were transverse spinal fractures, broken teeth and facial wounds. I felt a rush of exhilaration. I was alive. I wanted to be alive.

Mavis and Max stood beside the bed like two small sentries. They mirrored each other's body language, except she was pulling at her fingers.

'We couldn't find you,' Mavis said.

'You changed your name,' Max added.

I want to remember them well. I want to bright-side myself with an image of Max standing in the water at Waipātiki Beach. He wears loose blue togs and wire-framed sunglasses. His shirtless skin is pale and freckled and he cups his palms and holds them out. I swim over, and he dips his hands and grasps my foot. 'Keep your leg straight,' he instructs as he hoists me up and catapults me, weightless, into the air. Or of Mavis under a canvas shade rigged from the door of the Vauxhall Victor. She wears white cat-eye sunglasses and a white swimsuit. She is pouring tea from a Thermos and arranging sandwiches. She brushes the sand from the blanket and looks up and smiles. A real smile.

Then comes the rip tide that grabs my ankles, pulling me under, taking me out to sea. I remember a glorious moment, my eyes opened as wide as they would go. The ocean rushing in until I am immersed, unbodied in a viscous realm. And Mavis is beside me, dog-paddling, gasping as she snatches my hair and pulls me back toward the beach. Her face is a mask of fear, while Max stands on the shore, shading his eyes from the sun.

'Stupid,' he says when we come up out of the water, 'so stupid.' They do not speak as we ride home in the stifling heat with the windows rolled up and the smoke trapped inside.

I grinned at my parents. Happy they were there beside me in the hospital.

'We've called Bruce,' Mavis said. 'He can look after the girls for a couple more weeks. We thought they could live with us while you get better.'

Max left to go back to the motel and Mavis sat beside me. It was our first time alone in years. I imagined I could see all the words she wanted to say in the furrow of her brow. Why don't you grow up? A mother does not leave her children behind. Where did we go wrong? But we said nothing and I slept. They left the next day.

I called Bruce. The girls would stay with him until I got back. 'You can make up the time later,' he said.

Hampster visited a couple of times. When they discharged me, he pushed the wheelchair to the entrance and ran around to get the rental car. The harsh bright sun hit my face.

'You were so lucky,' Hampster said as he held the door and I angled myself in. I turned away from him, the gloss gone. We drove to Auckland under the covenant of high blue skies, and I thought about luck.

Adopted people hear the L-word a lot. Mavis's sisters reminded me at every opportunity. I was so lucky to have such great parents. A colleague once told me I was lucky I was not aborted. A teacher said I was lucky someone wanted me. Another mentioned how lucky I was not to end up in an orphanage.

The idea that we are lucky permeates the public discourse on adoption. Lucky implies that adoption saved us from all manner of unknown forces.

In one attempt to discuss adoption, Mavis was clear. 'Your birth mother's parents are to blame. You should be grateful we saved you when they did not want you.'

Gratitude is luck's sidekick. It's one of the hidden tropes of adoption. You cannot be lucky or chosen and special without being grateful and thankful.

Mirah Riben, who writes about adoption, asks if adoptees owe a higher debt of gratitude than those in natural families. Even for the basics like food, clothing and the care they receive. She details cases of adopted people speaking out and meeting online hostility for expressing their feelings. They're scolded over and over for not being grateful for their luck.

Riben calls it the 'duality of adoption'. 'You might have had a happy childhood. But every adoption begins with a tragedy of loss and separation. Adoption is a traumatic, lifelong and often unrecognised experience.' She describes how society clings to the preconceived, romanticised notions of adoption. The problem, she says, is when adoptees do not assume their role as grateful orphans.[14]

Writer Matthew Salesses talks about being in debt to someone's love. 'For adoptees, gratitude and luck can be trigger words. Society tells us we are lucky to be adopted. If we do not appear grateful, they tell us to know our place. We are reminded to be thankful for being taken from the mothers who bore us. We are called "angry" as a dismissal.'

Salesses makes the connection between forced gratitude and its effects on appreciation. He describes an idyllic moment with his daughter. 'I knew I should have enjoyed myself,' he said, recalling the perfection of that moment. 'But I couldn't.'[15]

I know this feeling. Somewhere deep down I am convinced I have no intrinsic right to enjoyment. Every good thing is at the mercy of the capricious, shallow whim of luck. Whatever you love today will be gone tomorrow. Every happy moment is a debt that must be repaid.

I have learned to never trust a clear blue sky. But over the years I've formed an uneasy truce with luck. I overcompensate. I'm always on time and never late. Every kind deed must be repaid, any gift equalled or bettered. I carry a mental ledger in which I tally every friend and acquaintance. I mark each for repayment or no further action required. If I leave a single column unbalanced, I am stalked by the fear of my luck running out. Of being unchosen once again.

We arrived in Auckland. Hampster had arranged for us to house-sit. In Ponsonby. I was on crutches, one foot in plaster, the other bandaged. The small spinal fractures were healing, but every step was painful. The bruises were fading, but my teeth took months to fix. This was not the Ponsonby of my dreams.

I spent my days alone, aching for my children and at the same time relieved for the break. Unable to walk far, I was stranded in the very place I'd wanted to be. Our host had an extensive record collection. I listened to music for hours, taking the lines of songs as my gospel. I wanted to shed my skin and get started. I wanted someone to throw their arms around me. I wanted to dance in the dark. I wanted the miracle of love, given freely.

There were books on Buddhism on the shelf, and now I had time to read. It seemed I had a 'universal longing'. A craving that nothing in the world could satisfy. The desire itself, the book said, was the source of my suffering. The answer was to forgo consumerism and to dump attachments.[16] I looked around at the book-lined house with the velvet furniture and the polished oak table. I thought about the flat in Christchurch. With the damp concrete walls and the broken coffee table. Consumerism was not my problem.

To the Christians, my sin was the source of my suffering. To my adopters, it was my lack of gratitude. To the Buddhists, it was my craving for attachment. The book said I would find happiness only by overcoming this grasping need. But I knew my craving was the thread that pulled me from the depths. Without it, I would die. I threw the book against the wall in frustration, and the doorbell rang.

The woman I'd met when she was wallpapering a hallway in Wellington stood on the porch. With her blonde curls pulled back and smudged eyes, I hardly recognised her.

'It's Christine,' she said. The brightness that so impressed me had dimmed. She looked so sad I burst into tears. We hugged each other, both of us crying. She'd had a bad experience. We sat on the velvet sofa while she told me all about it. She ran her fingers over the fresh red scar below my lip. 'I'll get my bag from the car,' she said. 'Then I'll make some tea.'

Within a week we'd found an abandoned office off Victoria Street in downtown Auckland. A bankrupt film company had walked out on the lease. We'll be squatters, she said, but no one will know.

I changed the ticket Hampster had bought and went to Christchurch to pack up our life. The girls drew on my cast and laughed at my broken teeth. David helped me pack. He arranged for movers to pick up our meagre belongings. We were moving to Auckland.

'I can stop you,' Bruce said. He could go to court, but I knew he wouldn't. The cost and effort would be too much. I knew it was wrong to take his children away. I understood I was hurting them by separating them from their father. But those weeks on the sofa had crystallised my desire. I wanted more. So much more.

Christine picked us up from the airport and we drove home. We had half of the top floor of a 1920s office block all to ourselves. Room to run and yell and play. We slept on mattresses on the floor and bought a hotplate for the office kitchen. We had six toilets and no shower.

Bruce's parents came to visit. I could see his mother through the frosted glass of the office foyer, her hands on her ample hips. His father stood natty and small beside her. When I opened the door, she ignored my plastered foot and strode in. She peered into the office spaces where sheets hung over the glass partitions. The girls had arranged their soft toys along the boardroom shelving.

'This is not good enough,' she said. She placed a stack of books on a table left behind by the bankrupt company. *The Miracles of Jesus*, a Jesus Lives colouring book and a *Little Golden Book of Jesus*.

'The girls would love some felt-tip colouring pens, next time you come,' I said.

I looked at these people connected by blood to my children and began to wonder if biology mattered at all. I thought about my grandfather and all the losses he carried and the suffering he'd caused. I imagined my mother standing next to me. Smiling as she met the other grandparents of her grandchildren. She would look at me and raise her eyebrow in our shared complicity. I did not want my children's sense of heritage formed only by these people. I knew then I needed to find my father. I would write to Jeannie again.

17

Your limbic brain on relinquishment

Jeannie phoned a few weeks after we moved into the office. She would be in Auckland for business. Could she come to visit?

She was early. I heard the knocking as I was getting dressed. Bonnie raced to let her in and came running back. Two women in straight skirts and ill-fitting jackets stood in the foyer. They were from the Department of Social Welfare.

'We're following up on a complaint of child neglect,' the smaller one said.

'We'd like you to invite us in,' the other said. 'We need to see your children.' They glanced in unison towards a white van in the parking area. It could have been for dog control or police work.

I swept my arm wide and worked to keep my voice neutral, careful not to spook them. They refused to say who'd complained, but I knew it was Bruce's parents.

I carried Ruth on my hip. The older girls were drawing at the boardroom table. The women hardly noticed them. Instead, they opened kitchen cupboards and peered into each room. They studied my shoes. Had they found men's sizes, they could have stopped my benefit. They noted the makeshift shower Christine had rigged after removing a toilet bowl. One of them handed me a card. 'You'll need to find somewhere else to live,' she said.

My fear leaked out. 'You can't take my kids.'

'Yeah, we can,' the other said, and she snapped her fingers. 'Just like that.'

It was raining when the social workers left. They were scurrying towards their van as Jeannie passed by. She walked with such confidence, oblivious to the rain, the two women turned to watch.

After sharing so much, this was our first meeting. Jeannie was taller than I expected. She wore trousers and a wide-shouldered jacket, and her dark brown hair was piled up. Her voice was even more arresting in person.

She held my arms and scanned my face and body. 'Pam's daughter. You could be no other.'

We sat on plastic chairs at one end of the boardroom table. She watched the children. 'Oh my heart, she looks so like your mother,' she said as Bonnie looked up and smiled.

Each time Jeannie said 'your mother' my chest constricted. I wanted to inhale every fragment of her. I wanted to know everything. And yet I was fearful she might say my mother left without a backward glance.

'It was all Fred's fault,' Jeannie said.

I thought of the frail and broken old man who'd died in a locked ward. Jeannie leaned over and twisted a strand of my hair around her finger in the same way I touched my children. An instinctual mother's touch. In those days, I slipped in and out of other worlds with surprising ease, never fully anywhere. Our psyche longs for narrative consistency. As Jeannie told me what she knew of the story, my imagination rushed to fill the gaps.

I see Jessie, my grandmother, patting the soft waves of her home perm. She and Pamela are sitting at the kitchen table, waiting for Fred to return. As if they know this will be the day. Pamela hears him whistling down the road. She had not heard her father whistle until they moved from Manchester to Tawa. The sound gives her comfort.

Fred's face is ruddy from the walk. He has tied the top of his painting overalls around his waist and his work shirt is damp under the arms. He removes his shoes and smiles at his family. 'Ahh, my pretty ponies,' he says, and ruffles his daughter's hair.

And then he sees it. The swell of her stomach that she can no longer hide. Pamela holds her breath, the possibility of his redemption like a haze around them.

Jessie slides two fried eggs in front of him. He looks up,

his eyes wide as though someone has switched on the porch light while he was admiring the stars.

Jessie turns away. 'Eat your eggs,' she says.

He holds his knife, studying the perfect yellow globes. 'Tell her. Tell your daughter to leave my house.' His voice is shard sharp. 'She'll be gone when I get home.'

Pamela has not heard this voice before, and it stills all hope. He sections the toast in precise strips and pierces the yolks. The midday sun forces its way through the nets. He gulps the food, then unties his overalls, slides his arms into the sleeves and leaves without a goodbye.

As soon as he is gone, Jessie goes to the hall. She makes a phone call, pushing the kitchen door closed with her foot. Pamela gazes at the yellow streaks covering her father's plate.

'They made her leave that day,' Jeannie said. 'Jessie had already organised it through her doctor. The one she saw in secret, for breast cancer.'

I imagine their house. The plain decoration, the net curtains, and the new suburb growing up around them.

Pamela places her suitcase on the single bed. She can't think what to pack. Through all the months since her mother found out, they have not spoken about it. She stands outside her parents' room and knocks as though she is a visitor. Jessie has left an envelope pinned to the door. The name of the doctor, his address and a train timetable. She has underlined the destination and departure time in red ink. Pamela realises she will have to hurry to catch the last train to Napier.

'Bye, Mum. I'll be off then,' Pamela calls.

She takes her case through the silent house and along the path. At the corner, she looks back. Jessie is on the front step. She lifts her hand from the folds of her apron. Pamela wants to skip home, but her mother turns and goes inside. The baby shudders, and she wonders if the tremor comes from the earth itself.

142

The train is full, but no one sits next to Pamela. 'Nothing,' she says out loud, 'will ever be the same again.' Opposite, a woman in wrinkled stockings looks up from a book, her face expressionless. Pamela watches out the window. She has never seen the New Zealand countryside. The emptiness chills her. Eyeblink towns rush by, blemishes on the endless green landscape.

The baby seems to be growing by the minute. Its limbs extending beyond the oblivious knot below her ribs. She has carried it in the smallest part of herself, ignoring the flutters and kicks. But now, on the train, it fills her with its presence. She has been living in a fog, denying the evidence of her own body. She curls her arms around the bulge and imagines the child already born. It lies calm against the curve of her empty belly, its skin smooth, eyes open and knowing.

She sways as the train lurches into a station. When she stands her skirt is so tight she can hardly walk. An old woman seated nearby clucks her disapproval. They serve tea in thick cups and scones with jam and cream. Pamela extracts some of the money Jessie had saved from her housekeeping. She sits on her own with the tepid tea and the dry scone, the cream turning sour in her mouth.

How much did Jeannie tell me and how much did I invent? I remember crying and my girls rushing to comfort me. Jeannie was telling my story, the one I'd had no right to, the one they'd written me out of.

Psychologist Paul Sunderland says knowing and understanding your relinquishment story is essential.[17] It's how you make sense of your later life. He calls adoption a denial. A happy-ever-after hope that buries the real story of relinquishment. 'The cover-up is that these children are chosen and saved. That they are fortunate.' The horrors of war, he says, pale next to the loss of a mother at the beginning of life. He says the idea that if you can't remember something it can't affect you is an 'old lie'.

None of us can remember those long floating months or even our first years. That's because the prefrontal cortex, the rational part of the brain, is the last to develop. But the limbic system is active before birth. Implicit memory, instinct, emotional life and flight or fight reside there.

Sunderland's description of the science of brain development makes sense. Experience *is* the architect of the brain. And it makes me wonder about those first ten days I spent alone in a nursery, far from my mother.

When relinquishment is your first experience, your brain wiring changes to accommodate it. This alters how you might handle stress. How you might process the world. It changes you. Many adopted people have catastrophic thinking. But we are so accustomed to living on red alert we do not recognise the formless dread as a condition. We fear abandonment above all else. Many of us have a heightened sensitivity to criticism. We suffer from depression, hypervigilance and addiction to adrenaline.

I am woven together and defined by all these conditions. Sunderland says many of us are expert at hiding it all. Often from ourselves. This, Sunderland explains, is because we have no pre-trauma personality. No experience of being any other way, of even being okay.

My personality and character as a fractured post-trauma construct? The idea fills me with grief. In adoption we talk about the triad of loss. The mother loses her child. The child loses her mother, and the adopters lose the child they might have had.

But there is a fourth loss, a different kind that no one speaks of. It is the loss of who I might have been. As a daughter, a mother, a wife, a friend, a writer. As a woman.

As myself. A whole life spent attempting and mostly failing to create a coherent self.

And all this time it has been my limbic brain on relinquishment. As if *self* is a separate thing, unrelated and always out of reach. Recalled but not remembered.

In the poem 'Lady Mink: A Sort of Requiem', Marylyn Plessner asks: 'Who hurt you, once, so far beyond repair.'[18]

I now understand it was my mother. But then Fred, her father, hurt her beyond repair. And I, in my turn, fear for the hurt I have caused my own children. Pearls of damage strung together down the generations.

Jeannie sat with Rachel on her lap, plaiting her hair. The girls had taken to her, showing off their drawings and their makeshift rooms. She had brought sticky buns with her, and I made fresh tea and laid it out like a picnic for the girls.

'Your mother came looking for you, you know,' Jeannie said. 'You were five or six. She was living in Sydney, in love finally, and they came to New Zealand to meet with Dr Gleeson.' She took my hands between hers. 'The doctor told her you were happy and it would be a criminal act to look for you.'

I felt a jolt of recall. A memory of the Onekawa swimming pools, as I lay sprawled in the shallows, the sun burning my back. A woman sat on the concrete lip nearby, her feet in the water. I could feel her eyes on me. She smiled and waved and I used my hands to propel myself towards her. I was almost there when Mavis rushed over, scooped me from the water and carried me away.

18

Sort
of
an
orphan

Jeannie postponed her meeting and stayed till mid-afternoon. We took the girls for a walk around Victoria Park. The rain had disappeared as fast as it arrived. And the sky was Auckland blue, the weeds around the park edges wilting in the heat. I had so many questions.

'How did you meet Pam?' I asked Jeannie. Whenever I said my mother's name, I wanted to call her Mummy. I rolled the word around in silence, feeling the intimacy held within its soft vowels. I felt I had no right to use it.

Jeannie gave a half-smile. 'Through my husband. The Wellington am-dram scene.' She described the world of amateur dramatics as 'wine, cheese and behind the scenes'. 'There was an indiscretion. Your mother, my husband. I think she only went to a couple of table-reads.' She laughed and did not seem at all bitter. 'For a while, I thought it must be his baby. But the timing was wrong.'

'You knew she slept with your husband?' Her calm amazed me.

Jeannie nodded. 'He was always hopeless at hiding his affairs.'

'But you cared for her after?' The words 'after I was born' stuck in my throat. That empty time, ten days alone, when I was no one's cherished newborn, threatened to swamp me. I fought back the tears. Jeannie didn't seem to notice. It occurred to me that those days alone in a nursery had caused me to avoid a stranger's touch.

'I did care for her,' Jeannie said. 'I met the train from Napier and took her home with me. She helped with my kids and she modelled for my brother who was trying to be a photographer. My husband was under quarantine. Well, they both were really.' Her laugh was as I remembered it from our first phone conversation.

We sat on a park bench in the heat. The girls chased a flock of seagulls that rose and drifted back down just out of reach. I understood then that I really had escaped from Runanga. That other life was over.

'She got a job. Air hostess with NAC,' Jeannie continued. 'She took the Invercargill shifts. No one else wanted to stay overnight down there. She told me she walked all around the town looking into prams, always looking for you.'

We followed the girls toward the swings.

'It was a terrible time in her life,' Jeannie said. 'In the end, it was a good thing she gave you up. You seem very well adjusted.'

I smiled and reassured her I'd had a happy life.

Jeannie lifted Ruth onto a swing. Bonnie and Rachel grabbed the others, and we stood behind, pushing to get them started.

'If only she'd survived,' Jeannie said. 'She would have loved this. Her granddaughters.'

'Do you know who my father is?' The words leapt from my mouth.

Jeannie became evasive. 'I can't tell you for sure.'

I did not want to beg. It felt shameful even asking. 'So, she never mentioned him?'

Jeannie ran her hand through her hair. 'A little. She was distraught at his rejection, but she played those cards very close. And he was married, of course. But she hinted, and when you told me your daughter's name . . .' She nodded towards Bonnie. 'I'll tell you if you promise never to seek out his family.'

I agreed without hesitation, knowing, even then, I would not keep my promise.

'He was Swedish,' she said.

I had assumed he would be British, like my mother. It had never occurred to me that I could be half Swedish.

'His name was Jo Bonnier.'

The name made me shiver. Bonnie with an R. When

my eldest daughter was born, there was no doubt her name would be Bonnie. And yet it did not relate to anything or anyone I knew.

'There's lots about him in the library.' Jeannie pushed Ruth higher on the swing. 'He was a Formula One driver. He died in 1972.'

Found and lost in one sentence. I would have been twelve.

'How did he die?' I asked.

'Racing at Le Mans,' she said. 'His car went into the trees and burst into flame.'

Bonnie and Rachel squealed as they lifted their legs, forcing their swings higher, closer to that moment of weightlessness. I tried to follow Jeannie's words, but all I could think was both my parents burned to death. Eleven years apart. He was forty-two when he died. My mother and her mother were forty-two when they died. I looked up into the canopy of plane trees and considered the possibility that I had sixteen years left.

'They called him the gentleman racer,' Jeannie continued. 'He was very handsome. I'll send you a photocopy I took from a library book. He's on a podium with a wreath of leaves around his neck. There were two sons. One of them is the same age as you.'

We pushed the swings in silence. I should have asked her more questions, but all I felt was a void where emotion should be.

The girls were hungry and Jeannie had to leave. She kissed them goodbye and hugged me. 'Remember,' she said. 'You promised. It would be too hard for those boys to have you turn up, out of the blue.'

As we walked home, the girls argued about who flew highest into the sky. I wondered if Jeannie had any idea how hurtful her comments were. Everyone was entitled to their heritage, except the 'well-adjusted' adopted person.

I did not feel well adjusted. It was a lot to take in. Swedish. Racing driver, dead before I had a chance to know him. Legitimate sons.

A few weeks before I'd seen the movie *Blade Runner*. Daryl Hannah plays the replicant Pris with a cold fragility. When she said the words, 'I'm sort of an orphan,' I was struck by their stark reality. Then Rick Deckard, whose job it is to exterminate replicants, administers the Voight-Kampff test on Rachael, played by Sean Young. When Rachael leaves the room, Tyrell, her maker, admits she does not know she's an android. He has implanted her with false memories. 'We gift them the past,' he says. 'Right down to a snapshot of a mother she never had, a daughter she never was.'

I put my hand to my chest to still the pain radiating from beneath my ribs. After, in the foyer, I listened to filmgoers enthralled by the special effects, by Harrison Ford's body and the futuristic sets. But all I could think of was Rachael's shock as she learns all her memories are not hers. She was staring into the abyss of her emptiness, so crushed by the realisation, she couldn't even speak.

Tyrell created Rachael to serve a need. Just as adopted people are often acquired to resolve infertility. Rachael was so like her creators; she thought she was one of them. In science fiction, this sense of being virtually identical to a human is called the uncanny valley. Someone or something real but not entirely authentic. And that's me. That feeling underpins my sense of self. To make sure, I took the Voight-Kampff test. The results declared me mostly human, which somehow makes sense.

Christine returned later. She was working as an assistant director on *The Navigator*, the Vincent Ward film. She described her long days as frantic, awe-inspiring and exhausting. The girls climbed all over her the minute she arrived. In quick time we had become lifelong friends. I'd even visited a lawyer to make her their legal guardian if anything happened to me.

As soon as the girls were in bed, I went to the bathroom. I wanted to submerge myself in water. But all we had was a line of toilet cubicles and a makeshift shower that leaked. I sat against the wall, listening to the tap dripping, and began to bang my head on the cold tiles. I wanted a singular pain, specific and sharp enough to overcome the nebulous other. I had no right to grieve the loss of my unknown father. His death belonged to his wife and sons. Just as my mother's death belonged to her husband and daughters.

Christine came in and stood over me. She wiped away a smear of blood from the tiles with toilet paper and led me to the sofa the film company had left behind. She opened a bottle of wine and put a blanket over our knees. I had no words to explain my nameless rage.

'You have a right to be angry,' she said in a way that gave me quiet comfort. 'You can't change what happened when you were born, but to also miss the chance of a reunion. That's painful. And sad.'

She talked about her father. Of his love and his emotional distance. Her mother died when she was eleven and her life split in two. 'We're all fucked,' she said, and we toasted the mess of our lives.

I sat curled up on that sofa thinking about the parents I'd grown up with. They were not bad people. I had taken their lives as my own, their siblings as my aunts, their parents as my grandparents. But no matter the words used, they had not considered me as one of their own.

We finished the bottle of wine. 'Let's dance,' Christine said. She put in a mixtape someone had given her and Leonard Cohen's 'Who By Fire' came on.

'Spooky,' Christine said as we listened to the music.

Cohen had taken the lyrics from the liturgy of the Day of Atonement. The fate of the unrepentant sinner sealed, his existence blotted from the book of life. And I thought of the mother and father I would never meet. All right then, I thought, I'm sort of an orphan. Pull yourself together, what choice do you have?

The girls woke up and we exchanged Leonard Cohen for Madonna. 'Into the Groove'. We lifted the children in turn, twirling them by their hands. We cranked up the music and spun around the converted office, around our joys and the pain that drove us. Dancing for today. Tomorrow I would have to find a new place to live, or they would take my children.

19

Your phantom baby

The women from Social Welfare came back the next month. I'd viewed multiple houses. One was infested with mice. Another had mould-speckled ceilings, and yet another had slipped sideways from its foundations. None was affordable. The women smiled their professional smiles. The smaller one suggested I needed to look harder. The other implied if I could not afford to keep my kids I should send them back to their father. They would allow me another two weeks.

Not long after, a television company moved in next door. The producer was a woman, the same age my mother would have been. I felt a pull towards her. She wore business clothes with flair, and statement earrings. Her name was Catherine Saunders. Every day I invented reasons to place myself in her path in our shared foyer until she came to tea.

I showed her around.

'You've turned this into a lovely home,' she said, and I wanted to cry. I knew how precarious my life was. I woke up most mornings with vertigo, my toes curled around a gaping edge. Christine had gone back to Canada to work on a new film. Mavis and Max were silent. I had so little money, three children, no family and no friends. I felt a humiliating desire to throw my arms around Catherine's waist and hold on.

When Jeannie had run her hand through her hair in the park, I'd wanted to do the same. I'd yearned to touch her hair, to smell her skin, to feel the safety of her arms.

I often wonder about touch. I remember the feel of each of my babies and their absolute softness. The little dip at the back of Bonnie's neck. Rachel's warm cheek, and the smattering of freckles down Ruth's spine. And later, when Lili was born, that tiny fold behind her ears.

Each of them sought me out instinctually, turning towards my voice, their eyes widening at the smell of breast milk. Their fingers moving in the air as freely as dust motes.

I try to imagine Mavis holding me at ten days old. Her new mother nerves and the stranger child. Did she clasp me tight or hold me away from her body? When the matron of the Salvation Army home handed me over, was Mavis's phantom child nearby? The one she'd lost when Max drove their car over a bank. The miscarriage that was enough to take away all her future babies.

In her heartrending poem 'Phantom Child', Emily Long says, 'I don't know what she looks like, but I see her everywhere.' She describes all the ways she is haunted by her stillborn child. 'She walks with me, every day, this child of mine who never took a breath in this life with me.'[19]

Today they would say I'd failed to bond with Mavis. Or she with me. I know she tried. I am sure she followed Dr Gleeson's advice to act 'as if' I was born to her. But I wonder if her phantom child visited her dreams. Like a secret lover. A ghost child who nuzzled her neck and reached down into her blouse to touch her breast for comfort.

The work of Stefano Vaglio explores the mystery of how infants identify their mother's breast. Olfaction, he says, is the mutual recognition of biological similarity between a mother and her newborn. It starts early in gestation and continues through birth, and long after.

It turns out there's a patch of sensory cells, the vomeronasal organ, within the main nasal chamber. Until recently we thought of this as vestigial, a remnant discarded during evolution. But babies use this organ to identify their mother's milk from the moment of birth.

I love the idea of an innate adaptive response as our first and most basic survival skill. It kicks in while the mother is still in a post-birth phase, before she has acquired the maternal memory to identify her child's cry or respond to her need. The baby leading the mother into breastfeeding, initiating the fourth trimester of gestation, as she inches toward the breast that will sustain her.

But what about adopting mothers? How do they bond in the absence of such fundamental processes? Today, the doctor might suggest the Newman-Goldfarb protocol for induced lactation.

The non-biological mother can force lactation through supplementing with synthetic galactagogues. Doctors often prescribe a drug designed for nausea. Some take antipsychotics to increase prolactin levels. Many go on the contraceptive pill to up their progesterone. Supporters of the protocol say milk produced in this way is equivalent to natural milk. But breast milk is a magical, immune-boosting elixir. It can change taste, smell, colour and composition to meet a baby's need, even during a feed. There is no evidence lactation produced using the protocol responds in the same way. Given the dynamic composition of natural milk, it's hard to know what they tested. No one knows how these drugs might affect a baby.

For adopted people, this protocol can be confronting. On the one hand, many of us suffer from touch deprivation. We have an aching desire for connection. We long for the physical intimacy of our mothers. And yet many of us recoil at the idea of suckling at the breast of our adopter.

And no, it's not the same as wet nursing or the sharing of breast milk in times of war and famine. The protocol is about a woman's desire to feel like a legitimate mother. To mimic everything the natural mother might experience. To convince herself, and the world, she has her own child. As if no other mother ever existed.

In the song 'The Whole Night Sky', Bruce Cockburn sings about knowing he made it too hard, and how every touch was a laceration.

That's me. I am a disloyal and transgressive adopted person. I know that despite her caring, her love and her desire, Mavis never smelled like my mother. And I imagine I never felt like her child, not really, not if she'd ever experienced the difference.

There is a word I love. Solastalgia. It's a neologism that refers to a deep feeling for lost landscapes. It's meant to cover the loss of the built world, or nature ravaged by climate change. But for me it expresses a longing for the architecture and environment of my mother's body. Her skin and hair. Her breath and, most of all, her smell. All those things woven into my psyche, recalled but not remembered.

Perhaps Catherine Saunders felt my desire. She hooked her arm through mine, took me on a tour of their office and introduced me to people. 'You should see the home she created next door,' she said to one young co-worker.

Her endorsement gave me courage. As we said goodbye I mentioned I'd be moving soon. I told her about the Social Welfare women and their insistence that I find a home.

She patted my shoulder. 'Everything always works out,' she said.

A few days later, she came over and held out her hand, palm up. 'Keys,' she said. 'A house in Ponsonby. The council owns it. If you like it, their rent is very reasonable.'

I stared at her in disbelief. She smiled and hugged me. 'The mayor's my friend,' she whispered in my ear. 'Oh, and I might have a job for you. We can talk next week.'

Bonnie had started school at Ponsonby Primary and Rachel was in kindergarten. I picked them up in the car I'd bought with my share of the marriage money — an old Vauxhall Viva with a rusted hole in the floor and doors that leaked in the rain.

As we drove down Clarence Street in the heart of Ponsonby, the girls shouted the numbers. As we neared 89, my heart raced. I knew this house. Hampster had driven me this way when we'd first arrived in Auckland. I'd noticed the three stucco houses in a row, their mirror twins across the street. Two up, two down, as though built for the old country, for immigrants longing for home.

We moved in the following week. The school and kindy and Ponsonby Road were in easy walking distance. Catherine sent over bunks and we set them up in the bigger bedroom. After months sharing mattresses pushed together, the girls did not want to be apart.

We started out in my bed, in the room I would come to love. It was Rachel's turn to choose the book. *Are You My Mother?* by P. D. Eastman. Mavis had read it to me as a child, my heart racing with the fear the bird would never find its mother. I cried as I read it now, and the girls buried themselves beneath my arms, they touched my face and counted my fingers. We were a very touchy family and I basked in the solace of my children.

Later, when the girls were asleep, Hampster knocked on the door and I let him in. He wore his yellow boots and looked around at our meagre belongings. 'You've done well,' he said, and tried to hold me against the wall to kiss me. He'd completed his divorce and was on the way to the airport to pick up his new girlfriend.

I pushed him away. 'Is it serious?' I asked.

He touched my forehead where tiny red jewels of windscreen glass still slipped through the skin. He smiled without embarrassment and dug into his bag and took out a small diamond ring. 'But you'll always be the one for me,' he said, and he glanced up the stairs and pocketed the ring.

I knew my children were an issue for him. He wanted his own.

'Thanks,' I said and pushed him out the door.

I walked through the house full of old-fashioned features like glossy green tiles around the fireplace and space for bookshelves. The doors were solid panelled wood. The laundry was a shed outside and there was an old apricot tree in the middle of the fenced back yard. I set up the stereo and put in a Van Morrison tape.

My ankle and my back ached all the time. But I took a pillow and held it tight, and danced around and through the two small rooms, out to the kitchen and back again. I was home.

20

Clarence Street forever

Apart from my children, 89 Clarence Street was the first good thing that had happened in my life, the perfect house in the neighbourhood I dreamed about. At night the streetlamp caught the leadlight windows. White gauze curtains billowed in the breeze. The stairs creaked, the house speaking to me in the sleepless dark. The girls found friends on the street and they played in and out of each other's homes.

In my memory, it was always summer on Clarence Street. The washing line full of dry sheets, the front porch bathed in the early morning sun. We had a succession of disappearing cats and, for a short while, a too-large dog Hampster had acquired and discarded.

Bruce was a teacher by then, quickly becoming the head of an English department. He kept his word and refused to help us beyond the minimal government-mandated child support. There were days with not enough food. But I learned to budget and save, and somehow the kids didn't notice.

One evening we walked past the bright lights and laughter at Prego. We stopped to read the menu displayed on a stand outside. I went back to my budgeting. If I ate before we went, we could afford a large pizza with everything on it for the girls and a glass of wine for me. It became our monthly ritual. We'd walk through the Tole Street park, the girls running down the sides of the skate bowl and up to Ponsonby Road. We always ordered the pizza. 'You're the richest poor people I know,' a mother from the school said when we took the table next to her.

A friend of Hampster's assembled a group of women and invited me to lunch. My generalised anxiety kicked in. Everything else about my life felt inadequate. My op-shop clothes and lack of education, my divorced-single-mother status. I walked to the café and watched from across the road. The women arrived in a group. With their film industry careers and expensive handbags, they were confident and assured. I almost turned and left. But one of them saw me and waved, as if she already knew me. Meryl sat next to me. She put a hand over her breast and I knew she had a baby. I liked her and wanted her to like me. We exchanged addresses and she paid for my lunch. I left the restaurant and caught the bus to the library, ready to break my promise to Jeannie.

The man Jeannie said was my father featured in dozens of books. There were photos of Jo Bonnier at racetracks, with famous drivers and beautiful women. In one he was standing on the sweeping lawn of a large house on the shores of Lake Geneva. There was a photo of an apartment with a racing car on the wall. And another of his wife with a scarf around her head, her eyes hidden behind large sunglasses. They were such beautiful people. I could not imagine myself in their world.

I took home a documentary on VHS. *The Speed Merchants* followed drivers like Mario Andretti during the 1972 season. I sat in my living room in Ponsonby and watched the grainy images from Le Mans. The filmmaker had captured the crash that killed the man I now thought of as my father. They were racing at 180 miles an hour down a long, eerie straight. And then Jo made a mistake. His bumper clipped another on a slight bend, catapulting his car into the trees. In the film, the other driver jumps from his burning vehicle. He runs across the racetrack towards the billowing smoke. The narrator, Vic Elford, says he saw Jo's car spinning in the air like a helicopter. 'It hurts when you lose a friend,' Elford says. 'And on Sunday morning, we lost Jo.'[20] For many years I dreamed of that burning car in the forest and the burning plane on the tarmac.

It took me months to gather the courage to call the international directory. 'I'm looking for an address in Stockholm,' I said. There were a dozen listings for the Bonniers, but no private addresses or phone numbers.

'I imagine they're unlisted,' the operator said. I was about to hang up when she suggested looking elsewhere in Sweden. 'I have a Kim Bonnier in Malmo.'

My same-age brother. Today they might describe us as twiblings. Siblings born at the same time to different mothers who share the same father. I lay on the floor, in front of the fire, the children sleeping upstairs, writing and rewriting to Kim. It was not the same as writing to my mother. I did not want to give too much away. Instinctively, I knew money would be an issue.

Meryl arrived with gin and tonic. She surveyed the floor covered in the failed letters as I explained what I was doing. 'You're terrified of finding them in case they reject you,' she said. That night we talked about love and children and enduring all storms. We talked about my two sisters in Spain and their life without their mother. And Meryl was right. I had been nursing a hope of reunion, a fairy tale of return, fraught with risk.

Reunion stories fill our reality television programming and our women's magazines. I've heard adoption reunions described as 'Oprah moments'. Mothers and daughters falling into each other's arms are good entertainment.

But those shows serve a purpose beyond tear-jerking spectacle. They help to conceal the real effects of removing babies from their mothers. They tell us we can step out of the closet of adoption without consequences. They assume that in reunion we find completion. As if on meeting a stranger the miracle of kin will wipe away all loss.

Psychologists call it 'the family romance'. A look-alike mother, a father with the same sense of humour. Their unconditional love filling the holes created by stranger adoption. Such a simple thing, blood connecting with blood, and everything is all right in the world.

But we also crave the stories of failed reunion. These prove the underlying belief that the adopted family is no different from the natural. That adoption is a better option than supporting a mother and her child to stay together.

In 2002, the Children's Society in the United Kingdom commissioned a study on adoption search and reunion. They looked at the long-term nature of restored relationships of 500 people. They found over 70 per cent of searchers failed to feel an instant bond with their birth parent. One in six new relationships broke down within twelve months. After eight years, 43 per cent abandoned the relationship. Rose Wallace, one of the study authors, spoke to the *Guardian* at the time. She said a surprising number of reunions stop after one or two letters. Sometimes after a single face-to-face meeting. She attributed that to pressure from the birth parent still grieving the loss of their child.

As an adopted person, my story is public property even when I choose not to tell it. On learning that I am adopted, the first thing people always ask is, 'Have you met your mother?' If I answer no, they want to know why. As if there is something wrong with me for not wanting to know. But if I answer yes, the next question is often a version of 'That must be hard on your parents.' Or, 'How do your parents feel about that?'

The sense that it is my responsibility to assuage my adopters' feelings is paramount. I must at all times honour the selfless care given to me. And I must find ways to justify my desire for reunion. The least offensive response is to say I'm seeking my medical history. The most offensive seems to be that I want an authentic identity. And the same rights that every non-adopted person enjoys.

For all the years of growing up, my mother was a nameless presence that hovered close by. She was the perfect ghost mother, emanating a bright line of pure love. Instinctively I understood the coercion heaped upon her to relinquish her child. As an adult I know how impossible her situation was. But in the weeks following her death, a small part of me relaxed. I would never need to confront that core of dread, the suspicion that she'd not fought hard enough to keep me. That she had let them take me away. Or, as Mavis said, that she had willingly given me away.

M eryl collected up all the copies of my letter to Kim and sorted through them. She selected one and made me sign it. She addressed the envelope and took it away to mail. I stayed home and waited.

Weeks and months went by. I became obsessed, stalking the shelves at the public library. I amassed files of information about the Bonniers, and their publishing company. They led storied lives with legendary family celebrations and public battles. I made meaning from the smallest detail. They were scientists, artists and writers, and they were rich. They were the opposite of us.

And then Catherine Saunders called me to interview for a job. The national contra coordinator on a Telethon. I pretended I knew what a contra organiser did. For the first week, I watched and listened, my senses on high alert, acting as if I was one of them, acting as if I belonged. From my first pay, I bought my first new clothes. A jacket, trousers and shoes. Ruth was in kindy and care, and Bonnie and Rachel were in school and an after-school programme.

I was a solo mother with a house, a good friend, a challenging job and even a car with a warrant of fitness. Mavis and Max were talking to me again. They sent much-needed clothes for the girls and phoned to express their support. They invited us for Christmas. The girls made gifts, we chose our favourite music for the trip and packed the car and drove to Napier.

21

The snob

Christmas in Napier with Mavis and Max. I had somewhere to take the girls.

We arrived in a heat wave. Max had cut down the tree in front of the house to protect the guttering. But there was a swimming pool in the back yard, squeezed between the garage and a corrugated-iron fence. The girls played in the water all day. There was a Christmas tree in the corner of the living room and a scattering of presents.

'Granddad, you could pretend to be Santa,' Bonnie said to Max. 'We could make you a beard with wool.'

'I don't think so,' he replied. On Christmas morning he handed out gifts. Clothes and pool toys for the girls, another nightie for me. His duties over, he returned to watching cricket on TV.

Mavis kept to the kitchen. 'You're our guest,' she said when I asked to help. I was a visitor, without birthright in that kitchen. Then. Now. Always. I'd left home unable to cook a thing.

'So,' I said, to break the silence. 'I've found my father.'

Mavis whisked eggs into sugar without looking up.

The week before I'd read a short story, 'The Imp of the Perverse', by Edgar Allan Poe. He says there is no passion in nature so demoniacally impatient as that shuddering on the edge of a precipice.

The smartest thing would have been to step away from the edge and talk about recipes. Instead, I stepped closer. 'He was a Formula One race driver. Died at Le Mans. Swedish. Did you know I was Swedish?'

Mavis was making a sponge cake to take to her niece's house for Christmas lunch. 'We've always loved you like our own,' she said, and kept her focus on sifting the flour into a bowl.

I gave her a quick hug. 'I know,' I said. 'I'm sorry.'

The girls came running in. They wanted to try out their

new inflatables. I blew them up and sat under a sun umbrella beside the pool.

I knew the problem was mine. I am a chronic over-sharer. Dumping intimacies in unwilling laps. Small bombs designed to flush out an endorsement. I wanted my adopting parents to be curious about me. And, by extension, I wanted other people to notice me, to take an interest.

I look at my kids and see snippets of me in an eye roll, in a comment or an exaggerated sneeze. And I wonder if this is what makes me want to know everything about them. To know them better is to know me. Instead, in my adopting parents' house, I felt their indifference. I felt invisible.

Mavis packed the back seat of their car with presents and her baking. She'd devoted many hours preparing for Christmas lunch. Max drove, and we followed in my car.

My adopted cousin's house was nearby. Most of the extended family was there. The garage door was up and the men sat in the greasy shade, clustered around a crate of beer. It was clear they'd started drinking early. The women were in the kitchen and the kids were screaming around the hard-packed earth in the back yard.

One of the men came out to greet us. When the others turned away, he tried to kiss my cheek. 'Come on, Barbie,' he said. 'Don't be a snob.'

I'd always felt at risk around him. He gave me a look, snide and complicit. As if he held something over me. He returned to the semicircle of men. Max joined them and one of them whistled and they laughed at something he'd said, just out of my hearing.

There were no trees or shelter in the back yard. I helped carry the food to a table set up beneath a tarpaulin attached to the side of the garage. At a signal, everyone swooped on the roast potatoes and meats. The salad of sliced lettuce and hard-boiled eggs remained untouched. The men took their plates back to the garage and continued to drink. There was pavlova and sponge to finish.

After the women had cleaned up, I noticed my cousins were missing. I found them huddled in a bedroom. 'This is a family matter,' one of them said when I opened the door.

'Our grandmother's headstone,' another said as if that explained my exclusion.

Part of me wanted to remind them she was my grandmother too, but I couldn't bring myself to say it. Instead, I scooped up my kids and left. We went to the beach and played in a park and the girls fed the ducks with leftover sandwiches I found in the car.

Mavis and Max returned hours later, silent and reproachful. I put the girls to bed and Mavis made tea while Max watched a rugby replay on VHS. She passed me a slice of leftover sponge.

'I'm sorry for leaving,' I said. 'But I was not exactly made welcome.'

Mavis squinted at me. 'They are not the problem.' Her cold voice had returned. 'They've always worked extra-hard to make you feel welcome.'

'They call me the snob,' I said.

She nodded as if she'd always known. 'Maybe because you act like one.'

'I don't like sponge.' I said, and pushed the plate away. 'I'll come back to visit you, but we won't come to another family event like that. They're all drunks.'

The windows were shut against the night-time insects and I started to sweat in the compact heat.

'I want to tell you something.'

From the living room, we heard Max jump up and yell, 'Come on,' and then, 'You beauty,' as a player scored a try.

'M tried to put his hands on me when I was fourteen.'

'You've never been truthful,' Mavis said. She used her

fingers to pick up a large piece of cake.

I watched as she ate it. 'Like a genetic defect?' I asked.

She turned away. 'I don't know, but I've wondered for a long time if there is something wrong with you.'

The transgressions of adopted people are a Hollywood staple. *The Good Son*, *Case 39*, *Problem Child* and *The Omen* all use adoption as shorthand for evil. The original tag line for the hit horror film *Orphan* was: 'It must be hard to love an adopted child as much as your own.' Even the Grinch's vengeful behaviour is explained away by his adopted status.

When we try to understand depravity in a person, we reach for ways they must be different from us. We look first to nurture. The murderer came from a dysfunctional family. He was bullied at school or grew up with drugs or poverty or a single mother. We work to place the blame anywhere but on the individual. Unless that individual is adopted.

In the book *Serial Killers*, author Joel Norris says of the five hundred recorded serial killers in recent US history, 16 per cent grew up in adopted families. This, despite adopted people representing only 2 to 3 per cent of the general population. These figures pop up often in the media. There's never a source reference. They lack time frames and qualifiers. Family situations, the age of adoption or previous placements are all missing.

Dr Tracy L. Carlis, a clinical psychologist who specialises in adoption, says many of us suffer from Adopted Child Syndrome. We lie and steal and fail to bond. We are defiant with authority and commit acts of violence. Many studies reveal our over-representation in a range of negative statistics. From juvenile criminal systems, prison and psychiatric institutions, to drug and alcohol rehabilitation.

We also have a greater chance of an externalising mental health disorder. Carlis says we are predisposed to become serial killers.

Whether or not we are good citizens, adoption unmoors us from our history and forces us to stand alone in the world. Dr David Kirschner says we live with sealed original birth records, and a childhood of secrets, lies and frustrated searches for birth parents. He says untreated, festering adoption issues of loss, rejection, abandonment, identity and dissociated rage are all normal reactions to adoption. No matter how well we have integrated into our new families, we remain 'other'. We are cuckoos in the nest.

And yet, our crimes from high to low are explained by our inability to assimilate. By our rejection of the gifts adoption bestows on us. By our blood. Thus, deemed immune to nurture we are instead condemned by our nature. And because we do not share their genetics, our adopters are blameless in our dysfunction.

The act of adoption itself is also exempt from criticism. Public discourse rarely describes adoption as detrimental to human development. We ignore and deny the primal wounds it causes. We do not dare challenge the narrative of the seamless exchange of a child from one family to another. Instead, we attribute positive outcomes to the wonders of adoption. Adverse consequences are all about biology.

What if adoption is the spark that lights the possibility of being anything you can imagine? Good or evil? Because when you come from nowhere, you can become anyone.

When I was growing up, Mavis assured me I was no different from a child she might have had. She would vocally deny her maternal yearnings at every turn. But I wonder at the impact of her lost fertility. I see now there was a fissure through her life. A dark place where she hid her true self. I saw it once as she held her niece's new baby close to her chest. Years later I understood her eyes squeezed shut and the single tear that escaped.

I want to believe that mothering was mothering to Mavis, no matter the origin of her child. But in her wider family there was a cold distance in the adults. And I took this feeling of unspoken difference out into the world.

I packed the car early on Boxing Day to drive back to Auckland as the weather closed in. Mavis and Max always make a show of goodbyes, waving from doorways and pavements. But today they stayed inside. Thick mist clung to the trees as we drove away.

As a child, I watched the TV series *Longstreet*. Bruce Lee telling James Franciscus to be like water. I thought of that as we drove down the cut towards the viaduct that swept over the Mohaka River on the Napier–Taupō road.

'You must be shapeless, formless, like water. When you pour water in a cup, it becomes the cup. When you pour water in a bottle, it becomes the bottle. When you pour water in a teapot, it becomes the teapot. Water can drip and it can crash. Become like water, my friend,' Bruce Lee said.

And I realised then why that one scene had stayed with me. I had become like water to live as the child of Mavis and Max. I had tried (and failed) to take the shape of their world.

I thought about the ways of water. I thought about the many forms I could become. I decided to defy Bruce Lee. I would no longer be formless. I would try to be like the Mohaka River far below. Relentless as snow melt, carving the rocks and forming the landscape on its way to join the sea.

22

The
cloth
mummy

We spent the rest of the summer holidays around Ponsonby. I had a new job at Television New Zealand. All three girls were now at school. I would walk them to the gates each morning and catch the bus downtown in my business clothes.

The silence from Napier sat behind everything. I wanted to call and tell Mavis and Max that I was head of contra on *Sale of the Century*, a new game show.

Early one morning, a registered letter arrived. For a moment I thought it had come from Sweden — that finally my brother had replied. The girls were upstairs fighting over their clothes, so I made a coffee and went to sit in the sun on the front porch.

> *Dear Barbara, we have come to a difficult decision.*
> *If you cannot accept our family, you cannot accept*
> *us. We, therefore, have no option but to dissociate*
> *from you.*

They had signed the letter mum and dad. And they'd added their full signatures.

The word 'dissociate' was a stone in my mouth. For some reason, it brought back a memory of sitting with a glass of milk at the kitchen table in Westport. I was almost five. It was dark outside. Bedtimes were a strict routine, so something must have woken me. I drank fast and felt the rim of the glass against my teeth. At that moment, I wanted to bite down, to see if I could break the glass. There was a boom of sound and my mouth filled with the shattered pieces. The floor moved and the windows cracked. Mavis screamed and grabbed me. She pushed me under the table as the cupboards flew open and crockery fell around us: 7.6 on the Richter scale. For the next few years, I thought I'd caused that earthquake.

The letter left me reeling. An intense pain radiating from

my chest. As though my heart had knotted around itself. I sat on the porch and wondered what my life would be like without parents. I had my children, one good friend nearby and one overseas. I had a job and a secure home as long as I could pay the rent. But where would we turn if I was sick or ran out of money? I'd read about a family of four living in a car under the trees at Point Erin, a local park.

I'd always known confronting Mavis would activate her fight or flight. I had broken the rules of the adopted daughter game. I had pushed us right to that invisible line and then stepped over it. I had caused the earthquake. I could not expect them still to play at being my parents.

When psychologists talk about Adopted Child Syndrome, they miss the core of it. We exhibit those dysfunctional behaviours to find the line. The one you can't cross over. The one where no matter how you behave, someone will hold you tight. It is an impossible task. Even when you are surrounded by unconditional love, abandonment folds itself into your helical heart.

In the 1950s the American Psychological Association published parenting pamphlets. 'When you're tempted to pet your child, remember that mother love is a dangerous instrument.' They said anything more than minimal affection would produce a dependent child. Rocking an infant was a vicious practice. Over-kissing (more than once a year) created weepiness.

In response, renegade scientist Harry Harlow asked: What is an infant's love for its mother? In 1960, the year of my birth, Harlow removed newborn rhesus monkeys from their mothers. He put them in cages with two robotic dolls. One was soft and cuddly, the other was ugly and made from wire. The wire mother had a milk nipple protruding from its chest.

The baby monkeys would suck from wire mummy for less than an hour a day. For eighteen hours, they would take solace and reassurance from the cuddly cloth mother. Harlow went further. Once he'd established the pattern, he rigged cloth mummy so that spikes would shoot out. Or it would grab the babies and shake them violently. But no matter how extreme the abuse or rejection, the babies came back. And each time they would do everything they could to make cloth mummy love them again. They cooed and stroked and flirted. They even abandoned their friends to fix their relationship with cloth mummy. The rhesus babies were attached to wire mummy for physical survival. But they had bonded with cloth mummy for emotional sustenance. Despite the abuse, that emotional connection mattered more than food.

Harlow showed that bonding and attachment are not synonymous. Attachment is socialisation into a broader family context. Bonding is the emotional glue that holds us together. As if our very existence depends on bonding.

At work that day, the contra deals piled up as I sat at my desk above Queen Street. I pondered what it meant to be a mother. Could I disassociate from one of my children? What would they have to do to cause such a split? I knew it was not possible. And I understood then that it was adoption that had made me an orphan.

Rachel's birthday rolled around. Birthdays mattered to Mavis. She showed her love with pyjamas and skirts, T-shirts and chocolates. She added ribbons and bows to the wrapping. The children loved to receive their gifts. There was nothing for Rachel on her day. Or for me on mine. Or the other girls on their birthdays.

More than a year went by. I was struggling to hold the

pieces of my life together. After-school childcare had pushed me into debt. Every Monday I flew down to Wellington for the taping of the game show. I hated being so far away from the children. One evening my return flight was cancelled. It took hours to find someone to care for them. We were all stressed and miserable, and I knew I would have to quit my job and go on a benefit. The women in my office seemed understanding. But it was the late 1980s, and motherhood was not yet compatible with a career. I also sensed their relief at having delayed their own childbearing.

The first few days at home, I lay on my bed in the sunny house on Clarence Street and cried. Our lives had never felt so precarious. I would write to Mavis and Max. I would apologise. I would ask them to take me back. I would be like the baby monkey. I would beg to be their daughter again. I remember the sour taste in my mouth as I wrote the words.

But then I saw Mavis and Max had given me a gift. They had done the one thing I had always feared. They had shown me where the line was, and there was a new freedom in that.

I walked the children to school. They were joyous that I would be at the gate to meet them every day. I walked on to the Post Office and, dizzy with sadness, sent the letter. I wondered if I would ever recover. On the way home, I stopped in a café. It would be my last cappuccino for a while. I picked up a magazine and read an article about a man in Paris who had written a novel while running his magazine shop. I'd always wanted to write a novel. I know, I thought, I'll set up a magazine shop. The border between thinking and doing is very thin with me.

My neighbour, the graphic designer Phil O'Reilly, agreed to help. Between us we came up with a name. He drew up a logo and I wrote a business plan. Magazzino would be the only magazine shop in New Zealand.

Two months passed before Mavis called. 'We've had a think,' she said in her warm voice. 'How about a weekend away?'

They booked a motel and we met in Rotorua. It was clear we were not to discuss the dissociation or my abject apology. The kids played on the swings in the grassy courtyard. I brought out the business plan. Costs and income and projections.

'I'd like to borrow five thousand dollars,' I said. I heard Max grunt. He would not meet my eye.

Mavis's hand flew to her mouth. 'Oh,' she said.

'I know it's a lot to ask. And I know I have no business experience, but there's a gap in the market.'

They were not risk takers, but they agreed to think about it. Max opened a beer and went to sit by the swings to watch the girls.

'There's a Valentines near here,' Mavis said. 'All you can eat for one price.'

'That sounds great,' I said.

A few weeks later they had agreed to the loan. It came with a lawyer's letter and a repayment schedule. I signed right away and went looking for a downtown location. I made a long list of every interesting magazine in the library and took down publishers' details. I made a deal with a local distributor and within a couple months the store opened just off Vulcan Lane.

The reality was not as exciting as the set-up. I sat behind my counter and plotted marketing strategies. I strung blow-up sex dolls in the window and hung a washing line of magazines over their parts. I balanced fishbowls on plinths with a goldfish in each. It took a while, but soon I was paying back the loan and making a small living. And meeting people as I grew into my life in Auckland.

Six years on from my mother's death, I'd almost put

aside the search for my family when at last a letter came from Spain. From my mother's husband. He told me about their lives, about my sisters' schools and their sporting successes. He said how excited my mother had been to meet me. How disturbed she had become after my birth. 'They bound her afterwards,' he said.

I imagined the surge of her milk, her body primed for motherhood, every nerve ending alive for her baby. I could see the stern matron pulling the bindings tight. And I could feel the ache in her breasts, her hope receding like the tide. 'She always considered herself to be your mother,' he said at the end. 'Always.'

I decided to go out that night. A neighbour would sit with the girls. A couple of women who'd come into the store had invited me to the bar at Hotel DeBrett, and I walked in and met a man.

23

Spooky
action
at
a
distance

I was early, sitting at the bar nursing a chardonnay, when he pulled up a stool.

'Have I seen you somewhere before?' he asked.

With the insight of that first moment, I felt his distance. There was detachment in the line of his mouth. He pressed my fingers instead of shaking my hand. I knew right away. I would go with him.

'Who are you?' I asked.

'I'm the all-weather man,' he said.

It was a good line. It made me laugh. I thought only of sunshine and beaches. As if his presence banished all storms. When he smiled, his eyes seemed to track me, to glean the right emotion so he could imitate it. By the time my friends arrived, we were a couple.

After, when I thought about that moment, I knew I felt safe with him, the distance cemented between us. In his world, you stood by decisions, outran them or faced them down. He was so sure of everything. I lay down in his pragmatism and certitude. And I got up refreshed, the knot in my heart loosened.

Later J let it slip that he'd sat in the café across from my store and watched me. He was working nearby on a television show and he'd followed me. It made me feel special, chosen in the way adopted people are always told they are.

He began to stay with us when he was in Auckland. He could be fun and the girls enjoyed having someone else around. Single mothering was intense and he offered a respite. He paid for basic things, food and clothing, and helped with the rent.

'We need a bigger house,' he said one morning. He'd joined me in the sun on the front porch.

'This is my refuge,' I said. The idea of leaving Clarence Street was unthinkable.

'How about we take a trip to Sydney?'

The girls went to their father for the school holidays and we went to Australia. J held my hand as the plane took off. We wandered through a downtown mall with gilded arches and designer clothing. We stopped in front of a jewellery store and he led me inside.

'I thought we could get married,' he said as we bent over a glass case of rings. It was more a decree than a proposal. I don't remember agreeing. But I loved the ring. It was my first piece of jewellery.

We married in a registry office a few months later, the girls dressed in blue. I gave him a weather house I'd found in an antique shop. A hygrometer. A woman in a bonnet popped out when it was sunny. Her other half, the rainy man, remained inside, his brolly at the ready. It seemed like the perfect gift for a man for all weather.

J insisted on a bigger house and he wanted me to sell the shop. It was not making enough money. On the last morning at Clarence Street, I sat on the porch and cried. With the store gone, I was back to looking for work. Auckland City Council advertised for an event coordinator for Pasifika. The new, multicultural festival would be the largest of its kind in the world. They hired me. One thousand performers on five stages in a park in the middle of summer. The festival ran like a dream. The stress was more than I'd bargained for.

When it was over, J took a short-term contract in London. I wanted to go too, and Mavis and Max agreed to come and take care of the girls. I didn't mention my half-sisters in Spain. They were grown now. Rebecca lived in Madrid and worked for a film company. She'd sent her phone number a couple of years earlier, but I'd never summoned the courage to call her.

I called Christine. It had been ten years since I'd seen her. 'Meet me in Barcelona?' I asked.

She was at El Prat Airport when I arrived. We stayed in a small hotel on las Ramblas. We drank too much and wandered the busy streets late into the night and laughed as if we were still in our teens.

'What time are we meeting your sister?' Christine asked a couple of days later, on the train to Madrid.

I confessed I'd not called her. Christine gazed out at the conical haystacks dotting the sloping fields.

I knew my lack of action was inexplicable, mad even. We were on our way to Madrid, the city my mother had called home. I had flown across the world with a two-year-old phone number on a slip of paper.

'But why?' she asked.

The adoption narrative says would-be parents long for and often pray for their child. They tell their adopted children they chose them. That this choice makes them special. That being chosen changes everything.

But, even back in a time of an abundant supply of babies, adopters had to prove they were suitable parents. Then and now they have to forge relationships with the fertility gatekeepers. With doctors and hospital matrons, with priests and ministers, and nurses. They have to open their lives and homes to the scrutiny of social workers. They must prove their parenting fitness.

It is your adopters who are the chosen ones. You were the next baby on the adoption industry conveyer belt. You could be any baby, from anywhere.

We use the word chosen to cover the entirely random nature of adoption. To brush over the reality that your legal parents are two people who did not know you when you were born. The only qualification you needed for adoption was your mother's circumstances.

I once brought up the idea with Mavis, that adopted people feel rejection at their very core.

She shook her head. 'You have no reason to feel that. We chose you. We wanted you.' It was as if her desire to build a family with another woman's child was her fundamental human right.

And yet a profound sense of rejection is implicit within many adopted people. Every baby separated from its mother suffers biological, neurological and psychological damage. Even those of us who appear to have no problem with it at all.

Dr Catherine Lynch, who runs the Australian Adoptee Rights Action Group, believes the compliant, well-adjusted adoptee has repressed their infant trauma. 'They have learned to negotiate and secure their relationships within their adoptive families.' They do this, she says, to avoid repeating their initiating experience of abandonment and rejection.[21]

I am not a 'well-adjusted adoptee'. In some fog-bound way, I knew I was so afraid of rejection I had not called my sister ahead. It would be easier to not find her than to reach out and suffer another rejection.

The train arrived and we started walking. I was in Madrid. The city my mother chose as her own. It was as sunny and dry as in my dreams.

We soon found a sign in a dusty window. *Habitaciónes una noche, semanal o mensual.*

'We'll stay here,' Christine said.

La Dueña was large and short of breath. She sat in a small cubicle in front of a grainy television. She counted our money, grunted and pointed down a dark corridor. The bathroom was at the far end. Our room was in the middle. It looked out on a blackened brick wall. There was no phone in the room. I sat on the sagging bed we were to share and felt my chest constrict.

'There's a phone in her office,' Christine said. 'I'll call.'

I retrieved the folded scrap of paper from my bag and knew I had to do it.

I went to the cubicle and pantomimed holding a phone, and the old woman nodded and turned away. She did not turn down her television.

The phone rang and rang with no answer.

Christine stood beside me. 'Perhaps she's at work. Let's try later.'

We walked along cobbled side streets and drank coffee and ate tapas at a bar. Men tried to speak to us. One put his arm around Christine's shoulder and in halting English asked her to marry him. We laughed along with them. I felt the pull of the telephone, so we headed back to the hostel. The woman had not moved. Her cubicle was thick with cigarette smoke. She did not even look as I picked up the phone.

The woman who answered was out of breath. 'Sí,' she said.

'Hi,' I said in English. 'I'm looking for Rebecca.'

'This is she.' Her accent was hard to place. English boarding school, I thought later.

'This is Barbara.' I felt sick. She did not reply. A game show on the television filled the cubicle. I wanted to smash it to the ground. 'Hello?' I said. My chest hurt.

Christine leaned against the wall. After a silent minute, she took the phone from me. 'Hi, I'm Barbara's best friend. She's your sister.'

I watched as Christine nodded and laughed. 'Wow,' she said. 'Amazing.' Within a minute she'd arranged a meeting.

She hung up and hugged me. 'We've found her,' she said. 'We're meeting her at a restaurant on the top floor of a department store. Tomorrow afternoon.'

I started to cry, and the old woman looked up and shook her head as if all tears were pointless. Christine took my arm as we went back to our room.

'But here's the weird thing,' she said. 'She hasn't lived at that number for over a year. She'd gone there to pick up her mail. We caught her at the exact moment she walked in.'

I have no memory how we filled the intervening night and day. I remember walking to the department store and taking the elevator to the top floor. There were racks of sale clothing pushed to one side and tall windows overlooking the city. There was an empty café in one corner.

The tightness in my chest increased. I stood up and sat down and tried to focus on my breathing.

Christine saw her first. 'She has your walk,' she whispered as Rebecca strode towards us. She looked so solemn and determined. She wore a blue pantsuit with a white blouse and pearls. I was wearing a light blue skirt with a cream shirt and pearls. I was trembling with anticipation. We hugged and there it was. That thing no one can explain. An instant and complete recognition. My little sister.

She stared at me. 'You look so like Mummy,' she said.

Recently I learned about quantum entanglement. Objects with no physical contact can exert a push or pull despite their separation. Einstein thought it impossible. He called it 'spooky action at a distance'.[22] But a few years ago scientists discovered that entanglement is real. Two particles, separated by light-years, can change their properties in response to each other. It is, the scientists say, as if an obscure communication channel connects them.

Despite this, science has yet to open its mind to the mysterious ways humans connect. To acknowledge the entanglement of genes, of our souls and blood. Or the random chance of standing beside a telephone in an abandoned house at the exact moment a call comes in.

24

Game
of
statues

On that trip to Spain, I read surrealist filmmaker Luis Buñuel's autobiography. *My Last Sigh* is frank and fascinating and includes his recipe for an excellent dry martini. And the best place to drink it — most often with his friend Hemingway, at El Chicote, a cocktail bar in Madrid, which Buñuel describes in burnished detail. The revolving doors and the polished mirrors, the mahogany bar as the altar and the cocktails as gods.

Rebecca knew the way. We entered the revolving doors as an elderly white-coated gentleman greeted us. Through Rebecca, I told him I'd come from New Zealand and held up the book. He stepped back and bowed.

'I am Don Luis,' he said. 'I am the boy in the book.' He'd served Hemingway and Buñuel, running errands, lighting cigarettes. He told us the great men were very particular, and showed us to the booth they always sat in. We ordered the exact same vodka martinis. And then we ordered again.

I caught glimpses of Rebecca in the mirrors that surrounded us. Snippets of me, particles of my daughters, a note in her laugh — it all felt so familiar. It seemed I'd always known her, my sister the total stranger. The distance between us dissolved with the vodka. My children were my first blood relatives. But now I was a person with a sister, another human connected by something beyond the imposition of adoption.

I drank too much and for a second, before the room began to spin, the world stopped. No one moved. As if in a game of statues, my old life was frozen in place as I crept up on my new. And for that moment Rebecca and I were the only people alive in the world, our faces reflected in the glowing room.

At midnight, Rebecca's boyfriend arrived to take us to the station. He'd removed the back seats of his Deux Chevaux, and Christine and I sat on the metal floor with our bags between us. We were catching the overnight train to the south of Spain. We had planned to hire a car and drive from Almería up to Barcelona. On the way, we would find my mother's home. We would peek through the windows of Cortijo Grande. But Rebecca had called ahead. Dana, her younger sister, *my* sister, would be there.

'She wants you to stay,' Rebecca said as she hugged us goodbye.

On the train, we lay on opposite top bunks in a crowded sleeper car. In the early morning light, and with the clarity of a hangover, I realised the weather house I'd given J was a bad omen. The little wooden couple would never be in the same place at the same time. They could not wrench themselves free from their sun or their rain.

'I've made a huge mistake,' I whispered across to Christine, and started to tell her how I felt about the marriage.

'I wish I'd said something at the beginning,' Christine said. 'It was fast and seemingly perfect, I did wonder if it was a courtship con.'

The old woman in the bunk below rapped on the railing with her walking stick. The sleeper car smelled of stale alcohol and ageing bodies, and we arrived dishevelled and sleep-deprived. We hired a car and Christine drove the winding way along the coast up from Almería.

We stopped outside the ancient whitewashed town of Mojácar. The cobbled lanes woven with history were wide enough for horses or handcarts. Four thousand years of families had lived in that town, generation on top of generation. On the walls and doors I noticed the Indalo Man, a prehistoric, magical god with a rainbow strung between his uplifted arms. As if hope was always at our fingertips.

We ate fried fish at a café on a small square and the locals ignored us, as though we were ghosts in their world.

We stopped to watch a butcher with eleven fingers chop meat with a cleaver. The extra finger, we heard, was a family trait, passed down for generations, along with the butchery.

The sense of history, of belonging to such a place, of coming from somewhere, squeezed my heart. We're tribal, I thought, individual but communal, somatic but part of a spiritual whole. Such belonging is understood only by its absence.

El Cortijo Grande, my mother's house, was in the hills above the village. Dana opened the door. We hugged and looked at each other.

'You look like my daughter Bonnie,' I said.

'You look like Mummy,' she replied.

The house was expansive, with a swimming pool and a marbled terrace overhung with grapevines. There was art on the walls and rugs over the tiled floors and shutters to keep out the heat.

We sat on the terrace with a carafe of local wine. In all my imaginings, I had not considered the purple wash of evening light. Or the smell of the wild lavender. And the sound of voices drifting from the valley below, the high notes caught in the sagebrush. We talked about my children and life in New Zealand, circling away from the core of our shared loss.

I was a different person in my mother's home. The place she dreamed up from almost nothing. The grainy images I watched on my grandfather's VHS in New Zealand did not begin to capture the allure.

The next day I woke with a queasy stomach and lay on my back in the pool, floating above the world. In this place of heat, I thought of calving icebergs. The crash of separation, the giant waves fanning out until they were no more than ripples. And the ablated ice mass dissolving in a new ocean, far from its origin.

Later, as we walked along the goat trails high above the house, I was overcome with a sense of being whole. Of being there and nowhere else. We walked on through the ruins of long-abandoned villages tucked into the clefts of hills. Their communal wells had run dry, their broken homes overrun with cacti and weeds.

We paused to throw stones into the shaft of a disused marble mine that dropped miles into the earth.

'Halfway to New Zealand,' Dana said as the stones echoed on for minutes after.

We stopped to rest under a twisted olive tree and marvelled at our similarities. She told me stories from their childhoods. The ponies, the hotels and the travel. Their father's wild life. As she recounted a car accident that injured Pamela's back, I realised it had happened at the same time I'd had spinal surgery.

I took her hand. For a moment it felt as though I was coming home to this fragmented family. To memories that did not belong to me. Everything connected by fragile strings. I wanted to slip into the middle of their lives, as though I'd always been there. I wanted to belong to this place. To be from here, my girls running through the house, learning a new language, growing up on paella and grapes.

We talked about our cousin. Her father is our mother's brother, Ian, the one who stayed behind. It was the first I'd heard of her. 'She's one day older than you,' Dana said.

When I suggested I might go to Manchester to meet her, Dana shook her head. 'I don't think she'll want to meet you.'

Dana grimaced when I asked her why not. 'She came to look after us when Mummy died. But she ended up with Daddy.' Dana put a finger to her lips. 'We don't speak about it. We pretend that it was normal.'

The family stories that followed our mother's death washed over me in a spreading pool of sadness. I felt a kinship. But no matter my warm reception, I understood that this was their family home. It was their family tragedy and I did not belong here. While we shared the loss of our mother, we'd lost very different things. But, still, that loss was strung like laundry on a line that covered the hills and valleys of all our lives, from New Zealand to Spain and back again.

I also do not belong to my adopting family. But I am bound to them for all my life and the lifetimes of my descendants. A stepchild can inherit from both step and birth families. Such double-dipping is illegal for adopted people. If our adopting families cut us loose, we have no legal recourse to our natural parents. No rights to photos, heirlooms, keepsakes or heritage. Our parents' death certificates will never list us as their next of kin. Our children and their children cannot trace their family trees, except through DNA. We do not exist in the record books. We do not exist at all, except as misshapen fruit grafted onto the tree of strangers.

That evening we lingered over a meal of fresh pasta and wine at the local cantina and tried to make up for the gaps between us. A butter moon was slung low over the Spanish hills high above the sea. I looked but could not see my guiding stars, the three sisters Alnitak, Alnilam and Mintaka. And then I remembered — we were under a different sky. Instead, I saw only olive trees, grey against my mother's memory.

Later, in the room where Rebecca had spent her teenage years, I opened a drawer. Inside were notebooks and pads with scrawled writing. My mother's handwriting, the long loops of her pen striding across the pages. Business notes, reminders to pick up the girls or book a dentist or a flight. She'd been dead almost ten years.

I held a sheet of paper to my cheek. It always starts with paper. We crave the provenance of words on a page. Of an artwork, an organic apple, a thoroughbred racehorse. A birth certificate. A family tree. Without traceability, the artwork loses its value. The apple stays on the shelf, the racehorse becomes a nag. Provenance is woven so deep within us, we hardly stop to think what it must be like to exist without it.

As adopted people we live with the unconscious bias of biological and cultural otherness. And often when we find our natural families we discover the feeling is the same.

I lay in my sister's childhood bed and could not sleep. The reunions had opened arteries of longing. My heartstrings frayed in both worlds. Later, I woke from a dream, from under a blanket on the back seat of Max's car. It was dark and I pretended to be asleep. We drove in silence, with the smell of Mavis's hairspray and their spent cigarettes. I opened my eyes to the glow of the cigarette lighter as the sun broke through the shutters. I felt familiar nausea and a tightening in my breasts, and knew I was pregnant again.

25

Land
of
light

I left Spain a different person. As though my polarities had switched. I had caught the tail end of another life. One that would never be mine. But still, if I closed my eyes and pressed my fingers into the sockets, it was almost possible to imagine.

I felt numb with the loss of my mother. And numb with sorrow for my sisters. They had lost everything. Donald, their father, had lost himself, his schemes and ideas half-formed and failing without Pamela. His heart was scooped out that day on the runway. Their wider family was mostly lost in the fallout from Donald's affair with their cousin. And the house that held their dreams and plans was beginning to crumble under the Spanish sun.

Christine returned to Canada and I met up with J in London. He was filming in a manor house in the country. Donald, the man my mother had loved, invited us to dinner. They'd met in Sydney after she'd left New Zealand, recovering from a breakdown after my birth.

Donald was the kind of man who engaged with waiters. He discussed the intricacies of the wine and where the asparagus was grown. He told impossibly tall tales that may well have been true. And he spoke of his daughters in a way I'd never heard from a father. His words brimmed with love and pride.

When J went to the bathroom, Donald put his hand on my knee. 'Leave him,' he said. 'He is not the man for you. Come back to Spain with me. Bring your children.'

'Is it because I look like my mother?' I asked.

His smile faded. 'No,' he said. 'But yes. You do. And you sound like her.' He wiped at his eyes as though he might be crying.

I could feel Donald's emptiness. And I wondered how old Pamela was in his mind. Does the person you've loved and lost keep pace with you? When you mark their birthdays, have they aged? Or are they forever caught in the weeks and days and moments before dying?

That night I told J about the baby. He seemed pleased. 'We'll make it work,' he said, acknowledging the rift that had grown between us.

I wanted to believe him. 'I can't parent alone again,' I said.

Something about the apartment he was staying in felt off. I was on high alert, like a cat with whisker fatigue, sensing air currents as if a predator lurked nearby. The next day he drove me to Heathrow and dropped me off at the curb.

Through the long hours of flying, I quashed my suspicions. We were having a baby. I thought about names and knew that if this child were a girl I would call her Lilian. The name I'd always wanted. An offering or a vow. A name wrapped up in flowers, purity and beauty. The name my mother had given me.

I lifted the window shade onto absolute blackness. The man I thought of as my father was still a mystery, existing through articles in magazines and books. My mother's footprints were all private, the echo of her life held by those who had loved her. I still knew so little about her. She was born in Stockport in the United Kingdom and grew up around Manchester. Her mother was taciturn, a woman who soldiered on, no matter what. Her father had come home from World War Two unable to speak of its horrors. I imagine that Ian, her older brother, had taken good care of his little sister. She'd had grandparents and cousins, too. And then they'd emigrated to New Zealand.

I took out the photograph Donald had given me. She is sitting on a stone wall in front of a country church. She is wearing slim pants. Her long legs are crossed at the ankle. She is stylish and young, gazing past the camera, just out of focus, past the unknown person taking the photo. Perhaps she is looking towards a graveyard or a wide-open field. According to

Donald, she was newly pregnant with me. Maybe it was taken the day she boarded the ship for New Zealand.

After they took me, she tried to live in Australia and then back in London. Then she tried Spain. She found herself at home on the hill above the Mediterranean. In an ancient place once occupied by the Phoenicians and Carthaginians.

Out the window, a sliver of sun came over the horizon and the land emerged from the darkness. The captain announced our arrival. I thought about being a first-generation New Zealander and how the land has embraced me.

Mavis and Max would be at the airport. I decided I would try harder to understand them. My girls would be there, too, happy to be up so early. I could already feel the pleasure of their bare arms around my neck. Their cheeks against mine, their excitement for the gifts I'd brought home.

Home. This land of bright light, of intense blue and deep green, of beach and bush and rain. Of humour and manners and customs I understood. This is my home. And, for the first time, I felt I belonged.

26

All reasons, preferably special ones

I returned to New Zealand, and my daughter Lilian was born. The marriage ended badly, as these things do. The next five years were a blur of toddler and teenagers. And then Tom arrived on a spring wind. He brought his daughter Amelia and his enduring love that has embraced us all.

I began to write — columns, op-eds and feature articles. As time went on Tom and I made three award-winning documentaries. We infused them with issues of social justice, blood ties and duty.

Two decades had passed since I'd first written to Jo Bonnier's son. I wrote again. This time he replied and we began to correspond. He'd fractured his spine as a teen and had been in a wheelchair for twenty-five years. He told me stories of growing up with a famous father and then losing him when he was twelve. Later, when we met, we hit it off, both of us thrilled to be siblings. We considered making a documentary. Together, we would go looking for our lost father. We would interview Jo's friends and F1 drivers from the golden age of motor racing. We held off testing our DNA. The reveal would make a perfect ending to the film. After many funding setbacks, we gave up on the idea and decided to take the test.

The results came in. He was not my brother. Jo Bonnier was not my father. I had not a drop of Swedish blood. We'd both desired the connection of lineage. The loss of that possibility sent us in opposite directions.

I was, as it turned out, 49.5 per cent Ashkenazi. A Jew. Tom, my husband, is Jewish. We joined a synagogue. The rabbi came to our home to marry us in front of Tom's ailing parents. For years I'd been aware of a Jewish sensitivity. Tom's Holocaust survivor parents moved in with us for the last years of their lives. I loved their world of books and art and music: the debates, the opinions, the importance of everything. Whenever Irene, Tom's mother, contradicted herself, she would shrug and lift her hands. 'Two Jews, three opinions,' she'd say, and it always made me laugh.

But there were no further clues about my father. I thought about the information available to adopted people. The 1985 Adult Adoption Information Act, touted as the answer to our need to know, was little use. It provides no more than a copy of your 'original' birth certificate. My certificate showed my mother's name and my first name. The area for my father was blank. But someone had added Mavis and Max's full names, their address and occupations. They'd included my adopted name for good measure. So much for an original document.

While I'd found my mother and met my sisters by chance and luck, I knew there must be more information. I began to write to the Ministry for Children again. This time I didn't beg. I called every week, demanding my files. And I recorded the conversations. A social worker said she could not verify my identity. My dates were wrong. Because I was six months older than my birth certificate, she was unable to release my files.

There are no new-baby photos of me, so it seemed plausible. I scoured the few images I had, comparing toddler sizes. I studied the moisture beading on a window and the shadow on a lawn, trying to link them with the expected time of year. After weeks of sleuthing, I realised the different birth date must be an anomaly. Or a fabrication.

Other social workers sent me off on tangents, knowing, it seemed to me, I would get nowhere. They passed me down to junior staffers. And on to departments within departments. At all times, I felt the staff were condescending, disrespectful and insensitive. They expected me to give up, slink away, swallow my anger and get over it.

In all, I had over seventy interactions with government departments. The result was always the same. Yes, they had my files. Yes, any staff member could read those files. But no, I had no right to them.

I run a company and am an award-winning filmmaker and writer. I am a wife, a mother and a grandmother. Still, I am not considered adult enough to read my own files. In the eyes of the law, I am an illegitimate child for all my life.

There were three further options. The Adoption Act says I can access my files if both my natural parents and adopters are dead. Or if I have reached the age of one hundred and twenty. Or I could get a court order.

To get that court order, I had to prove 'special grounds', a term created especially for adopted people. There is no definition in law. 'Special grounds' is whatever the judge of the day says it is.

Through a contact, I received a folder of legal decisions — forty years of adopted people pleading for information. The stories were heartbreaking, but the judges were adamant: adopted people are not party to their adoption contracts. Thus, they had no legal right to their files. In 1976 a magistrate denied an application by 'B' to inspect her adoption records. The magistrate said her desire to learn whether she had Jewish blood did not constitute a special ground. 'Disclosing information would open a veritable "Pandora's Box" of trouble and embarrassment.' In an application by 'P', the judge was clear: 'The psychological comfort of the adopted person was not considered grounds to open their files.'[23] Neither is a hereditary medical condition. In every case, the decisions read as cruel and callous.

I went ahead and petitioned the court to open my files. The judge requested I provide 'all reasons, preferably special ones'. He gave no hint about what he might consider a special reason. Would the anomalous birth date swing it? I argued that withholding my birth date was a breach of natural justice.

And then, a miracle. The judge decided in my favour. He released all files held on me by the Departments of Justice and Internal Affairs. I could come to the courthouse and pick up my documents.

Two of my daughters came with me. The court registry officer showed us into an empty interview room. He didn't bother to turn on the lights. I stared at the file he held out.

'Breathe,' Rachel said.

A few days before I'd heard about a woman who had been given ten minutes to read over her file before they locked it away again. 'Can I take this?' I asked.

The officer smiled. 'I'll photocopy it for you.'

We were soon out in the Hawke's Bay sunlight. I held the file to my chest. Of course, I was crying.

At home, I closed the bedroom door. I needed to be alone. I spread the documents on my bed and saw my name on multiple papers. I was Baby Sumner. Then Lilian Sumner. And then Barbara McG.

The desperate letters I'd written in 1982 were there. In one document I am called 'illegitimate'. In another I am 'the transaction'.

A report states my adopting parents belong to the Church of England. 'They are regular attendees at church' and an 'attractive young couple'.

Three weeks before my birth, a social worker alludes to trying to gain my mother's consent. Fifteen days before, Mavis notifies a social worker. She expects to receive her child that week. Another letter, ten days out, says, 'this couple is promised a baby by Dr Gleeson. They have been advised this baby is due any day.'

And then a letter two weeks before I am born. A district child welfare officer says: 'If this baby is placed for adoption, approval will be given.'

The words stop me. *If this baby is placed for adoption.*

Two weeks to go and it was not a done deal. They'd promised away my mother's unborn child and left her without support or options, but their coercion had not yet worked. Her three months of isolation in the doctor's home had not entirely broken her down.

But next, the adoption order. My mother's signature below Mavis's and Max's. I imagine her in their lawyer's office. She had no representation of her own. And I wonder if she signed without a fuss? All the fight gone out of her. Or whether they needed to steady her hand on the pen?

The documents left me empty. I gathered them up, climbed under the covers and fell asleep in the middle of the day.

A while later, I went back to the Ministry for Children. Even with a court order it took many more weeks to gain access to their records. When the file arrived, a staff member had redacted half the documents.

But I found the doctor's address. The place where my mother had lived during the last stages of her pregnancy, where she'd cleaned and served and held her hands over her tummy. I stared at the address. It was a few doors down from where I live now. The place I'd insisted on buying four years ago.

But in all the information, one thing was missing — my father's name.

On a whim, I moved my DNA from the American company to one based in the United Kingdom. When they load your DNA into their system, anyone with a match gets an email alert.

Within hours I received a message. I'd come in from planting a hedge of olive trees and I opened it at the kitchen table. My hands were still wet and there was dirt under my nails.

'I'm your third cousin on your father's side,' Jeremy from

London wrote. 'It's not an exact science. But it's possible, one of my three great-uncles could be your father,' he said. 'May I call you?'

Jeremy had a deep understanding of the intricacies of familial connections and DNA. His explanation went over my head, but his accent calmed me. There was comfort in his conservative vowels, a resonance I could not explain. He asked questions. How did I end up in New Zealand? Did I know anything about my father?

As always, I was self-conscious about admitting I knew nothing. The shame that matches secrecy beat for beat caught at my throat. I used one nail to clean another. 'The man I thought was my father was a Formula One driver.' I was acutely aware of my rising inflexion.

There was a moment of silence. 'One of my uncles was a racing driver,' he said.

Alfred Lazarus Fingleston, better known as Les Leston, born in Nottinghamshire in 1920. That would make him forty when I was born — my mother just nineteen.

Jeremy offered to contact Les Leston's son. He replied immediately and sent away for the DNA kit the next day.

While we waited for the results, I turned back to the distraction of research. I found my mother's address from the passenger list for the *Rangitata*. The ship departed London on 25 September 1959 with my newly pregnant mother and her parents aboard. They had lived in Holly Cottage in Bletchley.

With the help of a friend who has an uncanny ability to find obscure documents, we put together a possible scenario.

The Brands Hatch racetrack was less than two hours from Holly Cottage. Graeme Hill and Bruce McLaren raced there regularly, as did Les Leston and Jo Bonnier. In early August 1959 and again, two weeks later, they'd shared the same racetrack. After the racing, there were friendly cricket matches. And parties. *Motorsport* magazine reported the swinging sixties started early for the racing world. There's even a photograph of Stirling Moss in a bikini and heels with a stripper called Booby Galore.

A question continued to niggle at the back of my mind. I was born in late May 1960. Many of the documents seemed to indicate I had been expected weeks earlier, but my birth weight suggests I wasn't particularly overdue.

Two race days, two party nights, two weeks apart. A summer month of racing, cricket and parties. What if there had been two candidates for fatherhood? And a simple mistake. The wrong candidate told in secret to a friend. And that secret passed on to me.

Oh, Mummy.

27

You
are
your
DNA

The DNA took months to come through. 'You've struck a busy time of year,' the company apologised when I enquired.

Les's son Skyped and showed me around his home. He described it as 'our father's house'. He'd inherited it and the businesses Les left behind. The house resembled a barn, with blackened timber beams. There was an indoor pool and a circular driveway with a Porsche on display. My possible brother said he did not need the DNA to know I was a Leston. When we finished the call, he sent me a photo of a young woman. 'I'm so happy to have another sister,' he said. 'You look so like her.'

Another sister? Kimberley Leston was thirteen months older than me. She wrote for *The Face*, the *Guardian*, the *Independent* and other publications. She'd died in 1995. Her colleagues said they treasured her vivacity, candour, humour, generosity and optimism. They described her writing as deft, clever and fearlessly frank. When I learned she'd taken her own life, the sadness clutched at my chest. I grieved for her, my unknown sister, familiar now in every photo. If only.

But then the DNA came back. I felt the same seismic wave as when I'd compared my DNA with that of Jo Bonnier's son. Jeremy called and tried to explain. We were all in shock. Les's son was not my brother. My forebears came from Lithuania, the ancestral home of the Lestons. He was Scandinavian. Not Jewish.

We did another test with another Leston family member.

I *was* Les Leston's daughter. Kimberley's sister. But Les's son was not his biological son. The news was not well received. In finding my story, I felt I had dismantled his. I wanted to ask if, for him, the truth was better than living with a lie. If somewhere he'd harboured a suspicion? If it changed his memories around his relationship with Les? But like many bearers of bad news, I was no longer welcome.

Les had died in a nursing home in 2012. He was ninety-one. I'd found my father five years too late.

Les Leston had been born Alfred Fingleston. His parents changed their name when he was a small child. He was also known as Daddio, the jazz drummer in a band called the Clay Pigeons. When he died, Wikipedia and classic racing magazines and websites ran obituaries. There was a lot to say. He served in World War Two as a mid-upper gunner. He was a racing driver with over fifty starts on the F1 and F3 circuits. After racing, he became the F1 pit reporter for the BBC. He drove a red Lotus Elite with the DAD10 number plate around London. He moved to Hong Kong to develop his car accessories business and hosted a jazz radio show there. He owned a large cabin cruiser for weekend forays out into the South China Sea and rode a BMW 1200cc motorbike. In the evenings he propped up the bar at the Foreign Correspondents' Club, a bon vivant who talked a big story.

I often think about his number plate, driving around London. DAD10. Another small fact gave me the shivers. Two decades before, I had begun to write a historical novel, *The Gallows Bird*. It was set in London in the mid-1800s, and one of the characters was a silk merchant and tailor. He'd come to me in the early hours, his name and face clear in my dream: Mr Fingleston. I had described him as like an ivy bush of a man, small and messy, with a moustache drooping below his chin.

Jeremy and another cousin had created a family tree. And there was Mr Fingleston, a London silk merchant. There is one photograph of him — the real Mr Fingleston, not my character. He has a drooping moustache and messy hair — an ivy bush of a man. A platelet of knowledge slipped into my bloodstream.

Around then, Jeremy mentioned another sister. Lucy Leston, who'd changed her name to Teya. She was born

in Hong Kong when Les was sixty-two. I found her on
Facebook. We did the DNA to be sure. She'd grown up as
an almost only child. My sister, the same age as my oldest
daughter. She came to visit, awed by so many nieces
and their children. The children made labels to help her
remember all our names, and we folded her into our family.

I now had all the pieces, but instead of joy, the results
plunged me, for a time, into depression. Ambiguous loss,
my therapist said. Loss that occurs without closure or clear
understanding, such as when your loved ones are missing
through abduction or war or terrorism. At the bottom of the
list of such losses is adoption. You cannot mourn in public
because there is no defined death. As an adopted person, you
also have no *right* to mourn for those you've never met.

Over time I let in the spirits of all those gone before. The
sadness lifted, and I found myself at peace with them.

I am the *terminus a quo* — the starting point. I have begun a
new dynasty in a new land, just as my ancestors did when
they left Eastern Europe.

In this land, my children and grandchildren belong in
every way. I tell the little ones stories about their history.
How Mendel and Feiga Finkelstein, my great-great-
grandparents, fled from Lithuania not long before the
Odessa pogrom of 1871. They came to London and changed
their name. I show them photos of my grandmother Kitty
Fingleston. In one, she lounges in a deck chair, perhaps on a
ship or beside a pool. She has short blonde hair and wears an
off-the-shoulder top and a wide grin. 'She looks so modern,'
my eldest granddaughter says.

I tell them about my father, a bon vivant, a man who
flew in Lancasters in the war and raced cars for the fun of it.
And I tell them how my mother's bravery gives me courage.

How she picked herself up after losing everything and made an exciting life for herself. These are now my stories to tell. They are my inheritance, the jewels I am handing down to future generations.

I am still grafted onto the tree of strangers. My official birth certificate remains a legal fiction. Adoption laws around the world continue to sever the past as if it does not exist. I do not appear in my parents' documents or on their headstones. I have no right to their names or inheritance. But I am now placed within the sweep of history and I finally have a past. And that past lights my future.

I am the daughter of Pamela Sumner and Les Leston. I am the sister of Kimberley, Rebecca, Dana and Teya. I am the wife of Tom, the mother of Bonnie, Rachel, Ruth and Lilian, and stepmother to Amelia. And I am the grandmother of Margaux, Roman, Frankie, Zana, Dorothy and Fredrick.

I am still amazed I live so close to the doctor's house, the place where my mother laboured and lost. I imagine her sequestered in the attic — her existence hidden behind the tall macrocarpa hedge. Alone in a new country, unmarried and abandoned by her parents. A perfect candidate to provide a new baby to a childless couple.

I walk by that house most mornings. The doctor is long gone. A corrugated-iron fence replaces the hedge. But I stop for a moment and look up to those high windows. And I wave to my mother.

Notes
about
adoption

There is enduring power in the language we use to promote any ideology. We use words to align the myths and to hinder the truth, especially when it comes to adoption.

You may have noted I do not use the word *adoptee* unless I am quoting someone.

For many adopted people, the suffix -*ee* denotes our role as the recipient of the act of adoption. We are adopted as newborns or young children when we are without independent agency. Adoption is a life-changing and life-long event in which we have no say.

When you use the word *adoptee*, you remind us of what was done to us. Irrespective of how we feel about that. I do not use the words *adopted child* either. How often, when reading about adoption, do you see these two words together? As a New Zealand judge said when denying a woman access to her files: 'You are an adopted child of any age.' This term reminds us that our status as adopted people limits our rights as adult citizens.

I have also chosen not to use the words *adopted mother* or *adopted father*. For me it makes it sound like I adopted them. The suffix -*ed* is derivational. By affixing it, you change the meaning of the word adopt. I use the words *adopting mother* or *adopting father* because it places the action on the people who choose to do it. When speaking of adoption, I often use the terms *forced*, *closed* or *stranger* adoption.

I write from the perspective of the adopted person. No one sought our consent to be removed from our mothers, heritage and cultures. Most of us lost our identity without any legal representation. There is no mechanism to reclaim our original identity.

I do not use the term *birth mother*. This term is reductive. It's static and limits a mother to the action of her body. It denies the profound relationship a mother shares with her child. It obscures what happens to women who lose their children to adoption. It ignores the coercion many women suffered. It papers over the many social and financial issues pregnant women experience.

The systems and people that support adoption often ignore the impact on the mother. Mothers who lose their children to adoption can suffer deep grief. Many say it is worse than death because they don't know if their child is alive, suffering or thriving. They often suffer lifelong depression.

Recently, for the first time, British law defined the word mother: 'Being a "mother" is the status afforded to a person who undergoes the physical and biological process of carrying a pregnancy and giving birth.'[24] Let us call the woman who gives birth the mother. If parents enter a child's life through adoption, let us call them the *adopting mother and father*.

Others use the words *relinquish*, *give* or *gave away* in describing a person lost to adoption. But to relinquish is to cease to keep or claim voluntarily. We often hear that a mother *gave away* her baby. People are not objects. You cannot *give* us away. These terms ignore the fundamental human rights of the mother and her child. Every mother of loss I've spoken to experienced coercion and pressure to sign away their right to parent. Some of us see that as abduction.

Positive Adoption Language (PAL) is a movement created by the pro-adoption industry as a way of normalising adoption. *Natural parent* is considered negative. The industry prefers the more clinical term *biological*. *Real parent* is replaced by *birth parent*, reducing a mother to her biological function. The word *mother* does not appear at all in the lists of positive language. Even *reunion*, with its implication of desire and longing fulfilled, is out, replaced by *making contact*.

Language is how we transfer ideas or concepts. It seems to me that adopter-centric language is designed to minimise or negate the loss of being relinquished. Codified, the language disables adopted people from recognising and defining their experiences, and is geared toward adopters and the industry that serves them.

No matter how you view adoption, the issue of authentic identity always arises. Adoption severs the past and creates an alternative future. Some adopted people are quite content with this alternate reality. Many are not.

Adoption seeks to bind a child to a non-biological family. Birth records must be sealed to enable this. Authorities create a new or second birth certificate. There is no opt-out clause. You have no right to undo this action or to recover your original identity.

Everyone has a birth certificate. If you are a non-adopted person, your founding document is a straightforward affair. It names your parents, their occupations, your name, date and place of birth. In most countries, there's a small box at the bottom of the certificate. In New Zealand it states: 'Any person who falsifies the particulars on this certificate or uses it as true, knowing it to be false, is liable to prosecution under the Crimes Act 1961.' I have one of those birth certificates. It looks exactly like every non-adoption certificate. Except mine falsifies my details. It names the people who adopted me as birth parents. My name is not the one I received at birth. I am forced to use it, knowing it to be false.

I want an original birth certificate, as promised under the law, unendorsed with my adopters' details. When I complained to Internal Affairs, they explained the endorsements were to ensure I did not use the document to create a false identity. They went on to describe my post-adoption birth certificate as statutory fiction. And then as lawful falsehood. Later they described my original birth certificate as essentially ornamental.

The idea that adoption is now open is a misnomer. Open adoption is, in essence, an exercise in rebranding. Open adoption does not exist in law. Adoption is the same as it ever was: sealed records and a falsified birth certificate.

A mother losing her child to adoption may opt for 'open' adoption, but she has still lost all legal right to her child. She has no say over schooling or medical procedures. She has no right to insist her child remain in the country or that any visitation agreement be upheld. Adopting parents control all movements and all contact, even when a mother believes she has an open contract with adopters. Those who are adopted today have no more rights than people taken at the formation of the New Zealand Adoption Act in 1955.

In this memoir, I have stayed away from discussing surrogacy and the use of anonymous gametes. We use the language of human rights to insist that everyone who wishes to parent should be able to. Artificial reproductive technologies or ART extend the opportunity for people to experience parenthood. There is no legal need for a commissioning parent to reveal a child's genetic or gestation status. These parents are often vocal in demanding we document their children as biological.

Those created through ART do not have an intrinsic right to an authentic identity. The issues of belonging and identity are the same as for adopted people. In my view, we are creating a new generation of second-class citizens — people with fewer rights than their parents and peers and our wider society.

In the last forty years, there have been ninety-eight unsuccessful approaches to successive governments to change the law. New Zealand is a signatory to the United Nations Treaty on the Rights of the Child. We remain in violation of that treaty on multiple grounds.

The families of adopted people are as complex and diverse as any. Not all of us consider we have had unfavourable adoption experiences. But all of us must live our entire lives with a false identity and falsified documents. Everyone who loses their mother suffers some degree of physiological damage. No matter our individual experience of adoption, we are all grafted onto the tree of strangers — for our lifetimes and those of descendants.

I do not know what it is like to grow up without a mother. But I know exactly what it is like to grow up with a mother who did not have a mother.
— Bonnie Sumner

Notes

1   Jennifer Harper, 'Fetuses found to have memories', *Washington Times*, 16 July 2009: https://www.washingtontimes.com/news/2009/jul/16/fetuses-found-to-have-memories/.

2   *Napier Telegraph*, 'Bethany's future in good hands', 1978.

3   Hannah Devlin, 'Mothers more sensitive to crying babies thanks to hormone, study says', *Guardian*, 15 April 2015: https://www.ncbi.nlm.nih.gov/pubmed/26911697/; https://www.theguardian.com/science/2015/apr/15/mothers-moresensitive-to-crying-babies-thanks-to-hormone-study-says.

4   Deborah N. Silverstein and Sharon Kaplan, 'Grief Silverstein Article', *American Adoption Congress*: https://www.americanadoptioncongress.org/grief_silverstein_article.php.

5   Jenni Laidman, 'Adoptees 4 Times More Likely to Attempt Suicide', *Medscape*, 9 September 2013: https://www.medscape.com/viewarticle/810625.

6   http://nzetc.victoria.ac.nz/tm/scholarly/tei-Stout06-t6-bodyd1-d1.html.

7   Nina Darnton, '90 Are Killed as Jetliners Collide on Madrid Runway', *New York Times*, 8 December 1983: https://www.nytimes.com/1983/12/08/world/90-are-killed-as-jetliners-collide-on-madrid-runway-in-heavy-fog.html.

8   https://www.the-philosophy.com/pascal-heart-has-its-reasons-which-mind-knows-nothing.

9   https://innerwoven.me/2015/06/07/hiraeth-making-peace-with-longing/.

10 Maria Teresa Sotelo, 'Maternal affective bond scientific findings Review Article Corresponding author', *Journal of Clinical Review & Case Reports* 3, no. 5 (2018): https://www.academia.edu/39074813/Maternal_affective_bond_scientific_findings_Review_Article_Corresponding_author?email_work_card=title.

11   Iga Khazan, 'Inherited Trauma Shapes Your Health', *The Atlantic*, 16 October 2018: https://www.theatlantic.com/health/archive/2018/10/trauma-inherited-generations/573055.

12   https://www.brainyquote.com/quotes/william_makepeace_thacker_137822.

13   Zygmunt Bauman, 'From Pilgrim to Tourist – or a Short History of Identity', *Liquid Modernity* (New York: Sage, 2000).

14   Mirah Riben, 'Living With Adoption's Dichotomies and Myths', *Huffington Post*, 20 January 2015: https://www.huffpost.com/entry/living-with-adoptions-com_b_6504642.

15   Mathew Salesses, '"I never asked for this": On Adoption, Luck, and Thankfulness', *The Toast*, 25 November 2015: http://the-toast.net/2015/11/25/adoption-luck-thankfulness/.

16   Taigen Dan Leighton, *Zen Questions: Zazen, Dogen, and the Spirit of Creative Living* (Somerville, MA: Wisdom Publications, 2011).

17   ICAAD, 'Relinquishment and Adoption: Understanding the Impact of an Early Psychological Wound': https://www.icaad.com/videos/relinquishment-andadoption-understanding-the-impact-of-an-earlypsychological-wound?fbclid=IwAR33eqyAEronBcPJ7gz9i3ekljJ-YSdF3VYyNQiyUJc4RvFeuVrFbIGkWFY.

18   Marylyn Plessner, 'Lady Mink: A Sort of Requiem', in *Vapour Trails* (Montreal: Stephen Jarislowsky, 2000).

19   http://emilyrlong.com/phantom-child/.

20   https://www.youtube.com/watch?v=zlNe5pECpNo.

21   Dr Catherine Lynch, The Australian Adoptee Rights Action Group, https://www.facebook.com/AdopteeRightsAU/posts/-5-tenet-adoption-is-only-bad-for-some-adoptees-but-it-works-for-others-all-of-th/309553613039831/.

22   https://www.sciencemag.org/news/2018/04/einstein-s-spooky-action-distance-spotted-objects-almost-big-enough-see.

23   Judge Ellis, Family Court, Napier (FP041/31/68).

24   https://ukhumanrightsblog.com/2019/09/30/what-is-a-mother-in-law.

Further reading

'Australian National Apology for Forced Adoptions': https://www.ag.gov.au/About/ForcedAdoptionsApology/Pages/default.aspx.

Brodzinsky, David M., and Marshall D. Schechter (eds). *The Psychology of Adoption*. Oxford: Oxford University Press, 1979.

'Historical Trauma and Aboriginal Healing'. Aboriginal Healing Foundation, Ontario, Canada. Email: programs@ahf.ca.

Lynch, Catherine M. 'Campaign for Adoptee Equality, Adoptee Manifesto': https://www.academia.edu/26367687/Adoptee_Manifesto.docx.

———— *An Ado/aptive Reading and Writing of Australia and its Contemporary Literature*. Sydney: University of Sydney, 2007.

Meyers, Kit. *Rethinking 'Positive' Adoption Language and Reclaiming Stigmatized Identities*: https://www.academia.edu/5655199/_Rethinking_Positive_Adoption_Language_and_Reclaiming_Stigmatized_Identities_.

Orman, Meghann. *Adoption, Genealogical Bewilderment and Biological Heritage Bricolage*. Wageningen: Wageningen University & Research, The Netherlands, 2018.

'The Adoptee Journey — The Battle to Emerge: Resource Collection': https://louisaleontiades.com/the-battle-to-emerge-resource-collection/.

Verrier, Nancy. *The Primal Wound: Understanding the Adopted Child*. Nancy Verrier, 2003.

Wolf Small, Joanne. *The Adoption Mystique: A Hard Hitting Exposé of the Powerful Negative Social Stigma that Permeates Child Adoption in the United States*. Authorhouse, 2007.

Acknowledgements

How do you thank someone who gives his everything? And then some. Thomas Burstyn, a man made for marriage. I will love you till my last breath.

My daughters shape my world. Because of them, the sun rises. Bonnie, Rachel, Ruth, Lili and Amelia, I love you.

My hope is that my grandchildren inherit a more enlightened future.

Meryl Canestri read every word, chapter by chapter. I couldn't have done it without you. Nicola Legat believed in me and supported this work from the first couple of chapters. Jane Parkin edited with finesse and sensitivity. Ken Duncum gave wise encouragement. Renée read an early draft. Her enthusiasm kept me going.

Throughout the writing, Michael Talbot-Kelly helped me keep my balance. And Ron Law answered every panicked email with his scarily good research skills. Finally, my gratitude to lawyer Robert Ludbrook. No one in New Zealand has given so much and done so much to overturn the archaic 1955 Adoption Act.

To all of us affected by forced, secret, stranger adoption — may we all find home.

Author's note

All quotes used in this memoir are an aggregation of memory. Some names have been changed out of sensitivity to those concerned.